Spotlight on Young Children

Exploring
Language & Literacy

Amy Shillady, editor

National Association for the Education of Young Children
Washington, DC

National Association for the Education of Young Children
1313 L Street NW, Suite 500
Washington, DC 20005-4101
202-232-8777 • 800-424-2460
www.naeyc.org

NAEYC Books

Chief Publishing Officer
Derry Koralek

Editor-in-Chief
Kathy Charner

Director of Creative Services
Edwin C. Malstrom

Managing Editor
Mary Jaffe

Senior Editor
Holly Bohart

Senior Graphic Designer
Malini Dominey

Associate Editor
Elizabeth Wegner

Editorial Assistant
Ryan Smith

Contributing Editors

Senior Editor
Catherine Cauman

Associate Editor
Denni Johnson

Assistant Editor
Mabel Yu

Through its publications program, the National Association for the Education of Young Children (NAEYC) provides a forum for discussion of major issues and ideas in the early childhood field, with the hope of provoking thought and promoting professional growth. The views expressed or implied in this book are not necessarily those of the Association or its members.

The following are selections published previously in *Young Children* and the issues in which they appeared: J.A. Hansen, "First Grade Writers Revisit Their Work," January 2007; N.K. Duke, "Let's Look in a Book! Using Nonfiction Reference Materials With Young Children," May 2007; R. Shagoury, "Language to Language: Nurturing Writing Development in Multilingual Classrooms," March 2009; B.A. Marinak, M.J. Strickland, and J.B. Keat, "A Mosaic of Words: Using Photo-Narration to Support All Learners," September 2010; C.A. Elster, "'Snow on My Eyelashes'—Language Awareness Through Age-Appropriate Poetry Experiences," September 2010; C. Gillanders and D.C. Castro, "Storybook Reading for Young Dual Language Learners," January 2011; D. Zambo, "Young Girls Discovering Their Voice With Literacy and Readers Theater," March 2011; J.M. Huffman and C. Fortenberry, "Helping Preschoolers Prepare for Writing: Developing Fine Motor Skills," September 2011; N. Darling-Kuria, "What Do We Mean by Reading Readiness?," January 2012; N. Stockall and L.R. Dennis, "The Daily Dozen: Strategies for Enhancing Social Communication of Infants With Language Delays," September 2012; M.F. Collins, "Sagacious, Sophisticated, and Sedulous: The Importance of Discussing 50-Cent Words With Preschoolers," November 2012; M.P. Ghiso, "Every Language Is Special: Promoting Dual Language Learning in Multicultural Primary Schools," March 2013.

Permissions

Poem excerpts in the article "'Snow on My Eyelashes'— Language Awareness Through Age-Appropriate Poetry Experiences" on pages 72–81 are printed, with permission, from E. Merriam, *YOU BE GOOD & I'LL BE NIGHT* (New York: HarperTrophy, 1996).

Information in the table Activities That Promote Fine Motor Development on page 24 is adapted, with permission, from N.R. Carvell, *Language Enrichment Activities Program (LEAP),* vol. 1 (Dallas, TX: Southern Methodist University, 2006).

Photo Credits

Courtesy of article authors: 3–7; 23; 28; 34, 36; 52–55 (children's work samples); 65–70 (children's work samples); 92–94 (children's work samples)

Copyright © Laura J. Colker: 69; Julia Luckenbill: 10, 13; NAEYC: 22, 41; © NAEYC/Barbara Bent: 30; © NAEYC/Susan Woog Wagner: 25; Elisabeth Nichols: 61; Karen Phillips: 17, 21; Shari Schmidt: 26; Ellen B. Senisi: cover photos, 48, 57, 60, 64, 72, 76, 78, 82, 87, 91; James Whitney: 51, 52, 53, 56; Susan Woog Wagner: 14

Credits

Cover design: Edwin C. Malstrom

Spotlight on Young Children: Exploring Language and Literacy.

Library of Congress Control Number: 2014939178
ISBN: 978-1-938113-05-5
Item 2830

Contents

The book closes with a study guide by Sue Mankiw that poses questions to expand on the content of each article. Readers can reflect on the questions alone, talk about them with colleagues, or discuss them as participants in a class or workshop led by a facilitator. The guide begins with "Recalling Your Own Early Experiences," which asks readers to think about their own language and literacy experiences. The section "Expanding on Each Article" includes a brief summary of each article and specific questions and follow-up activities. In the last section of the study guide, "Making Connections," readers consider the big picture, examine their curricula and ways to improve their teaching practices, plan ways to involve families, and identify next steps.

Introduction

Nell K. Duke

Rashaad begins the day by reading two texts aloud to the children. Because they will soon be planting a class garden, he first reads a short informational piece about turnips, a vegetable he thinks may be unfamiliar to the children. Then he reads aloud a storybook in which turnips figure prominently. As the children listen to the story, Rashaad stops several times to make connections to the information they are hearing, point out salient print in the book, briefly explain new vocabulary, and ask them to think about what has happened in the story so far and what might happen next. Sometimes these are whole-class discussions. Other times he has children turn and talk to a partner using a social interaction approach called *think-pair-share*—children think about their response to a question, pair up with a child sitting near them, and take turns sharing their thinking. Rashaad encourages children who speak a language other than English at home to use that language, as well as English, during the think-pair-share time.

Mountains of research suggest that Rashaad's strategies will promote children's language and literacy development, including their basic understandings about how print works, their vocabulary knowledge, and their comprehension (e.g., Beck & McKeown 2007; Culatta, Hall-Kenyon, & Black 2010; Piasta et al. 2012). This book is about how to help us all be rich developers of young children's language and literacy.

One of the notable features of this compilation is that it helps us think about promoting children's language and literacy skills early—during the infant and toddler years. This is well justified. Numerous studies suggest that the quality of language experiences in the earliest years of life affects children's later language development (e.g., Hart & Risley 1995; Hadley et al. 2011). The content in this collection continues through the second and third grade years. Such focus is critical, as children's language and literacy skills in these grades predict later literacy achievement (e.g., Nation & Snowling 2004; Catts et al. 2012).

The articles focus on many aspects of language and literacy development, including oral language, reading, and writing. All are critical, and they work synergistically in children's development. For example, exposure to the word *sprout* during several types of activities—such as read-alouds, discussions as children observe their growing garden, and science journal labeling activities—is more likely to result in deeper understanding of this word than if it is used in only one context or modality.

The articles cover different kinds of text, including stories, informational texts, and poetry. Research shows that young children can thrive with these types of text and that each can be developmentally appropriate for young children (Watanabe & Duke 2013). Articles also focus on the strengths and needs of dual language learners as well as those of children who are monolingual. This too is important, as research strongly supports the use of young children's home languages as a bridge to learning additional languages (August & Shanahan 2006).

Fostering children's language and literacy development is one of the most important roles for early childhood educators, for these skills help prepare children to succeed in school and beyond. I hope the ideas in this book will both guide and inspire you.

Nell K. Duke, EdD, is a professor of literacy, language, and culture and a faculty affiliate for the combined program in education and psychology at the University of Michigan.

Nancy Stockall and Lindsay R. Dennis, in "The Daily Dozen: Strategies for Enhancing Social Communication of Infants With Language Delays," describe early language strategies that are appropriate for all infants but are critical for those with developmental delays.

In "What Do We Mean by Reading Readiness?," Nikki Darling-Kuria describes strategies for communicating and working with families to promote developmentally appropriate ways to support infants' and toddlers' literacy development.

"Sagacious, Sophisticated, and Sedulous: The Importance of Discussing 50-Cent Words With Preschoolers," by Molly F. Collins, describes how to strengthen preschoolers' vocabulary by initiating conversations about high-level words during storybook readings, conversations, and classroom activities.

In "Helping Children Prepare for Writing: Developing Fine Motor Skills," J. Michelle Huffman and Callie Fortenberry explain the four developmental stages of fine motor development and how they help prepare preschoolers for writing. A table suggests activities and materials teachers can use to promote this development.

Barbara A. Marinak, Martha J. Strickland, and Jane Blakely Keat, authors of "Using Photo-Narration to Support the Language Development of All Learners," describe preschool teachers' use of photo-narration and the language experience approach to support the language development of young children learning English. By talking one-on-one with children about photos of the children's home lives, teachers connect with children and their families and cultures.

Cristina Gillanders and Dina C. Castro describe how reading storybooks aloud with children promotes the language and literacy development of preschool dual language learners. Their article, "Storybook Reading for Young Dual Language Learners," includes strategies for English-speaking teachers and a storybook-reading lesson plan.

In "Vivian Paley's Storytelling/Story Acting Comes to the Boston Public Schools," Ben Mardell, Marina Boni, and Jason Sachs highlight storyteller and author Vivian Paley, whose work provides the foundation for storytelling/story acting (ST/SA) in 50 Boston kindergarten classrooms. The authors describe how ST/SA promotes language and literacy and how to adapt it to meet children's diverse needs.

Ruth Shagoury is a university literacy researcher who spent several years in a multilingual kindergarten classroom where six different languages were represented. In "Language to Language: Nurturing Writing Development in Multilingual Classrooms," she shows how teachers can support the pre-writing and writing skills of dual language learners.

Nell K. Duke's "Let's Look in a Book! Using Nonfiction Reference Materials With Young Children" explains the benefits of using reference materials to promote first grade children's literacy skills. By encouraging children to use these materials to find answers to their questions and by integrating reference materials into everyday activities, teachers also build children's knowledge of the world.

In "First Grade Writers Revisit Their Work," Jane A. Hansen describes a community of children as they gain language and literacy skills through writers' workshops. With support from the teacher, children evaluate their own work, reviewing and revising their text and illustrations to ensure that their messages are clear.

Charles A. Elster describes how age-appropriate poetry experiences promote first and second grade children's language awareness in "'Snow on My Eyelashes'—Language Awareness Through Age-Appropriate Poetry Experiences." He illustrates ways teachers can use poetry to support children's awareness of sounds, letters, and word meanings.

Debby Zambo's "Young Girls Discovering Their Voice With Literacy and Readers Theater" describes how Readers Theater—cooperative dramatic reading from a text—enables second grade girls to find their own voice as they absorb and speak the words of strong female characters. Zambo illustrates how this strategy can reduce relational aggression among girls.

In "Every Language Is Special: Promoting Dual Language Learning in Multicultural Primary Schools," María Paula Ghiso writes about a summer program for second- and third-graders in a school district that serves children from 69 countries. She describes ways to support children's acquisition of English skills and to value and build on their home languages and cultures.

References

August, D., & T. Shanahan, eds. 2006. *Developing Literacy in Second-Language Learners: Report of the National Literacy Panel on Language-Minority Children and Youth.* Mahwah, NJ: Erlbaum.

Beck, I.L., & M.G. McKeown. 2007. "Increasing Young Low-Income Children's Oral Vocabulary Repertoires Through Rich and Focused Instruction." *The Elementary School Journal* 107 (3): 251–71.

Catts, H.W., D. Compton, J.B. Tomblin, & M.S. Bridges. 2012. "Prevalence and Nature of Late-Emerging Poor Readers." *Journal of Educational Psychology* 104 (1): 166–81.

Culatta, B., K.M. Hall-Kenyon, & S. Black. 2010. "Teaching Expository Comprehension Skills in Early Childhood Classrooms." *Topics in Language Disorders* 30 (4): 323–38.

Hadley, P.A., M. Rispoli, C. Fitzgerald, & A. Bahnsen. 2011. "Predictors of Morphosyntactic Growth in Typically Developing Toddlers: Contributions of Parent Input and Child Sex." *Journal of Speech, Language, and Hearing Research* 54 (2): 549–66.

Hart, B., & T.R. Risley. 1995. *Meaningful Differences in the Everyday Experience of Young American Children.* Baltimore, MD: Brookes.

Nation, K., & M.J. Snowling. 2004. "Beyond Phonological Skills: Broader Language Skills Contribute to the Development of Reading." *Journal of Research in Reading* 27 (4): 342–56.

Piasta, S.B., L.M. Justice, A.S. McGinty, & J.N. Kaderavek. 2012. "Increasing Young Children's Contact With Print During Shared Reading: Longitudinal Effects on Literacy Achievement." *Child Development* 83 (3): 810–20.

Watanabe, L.M., & N.K. Duke. 2013. "Read All About I.T.! Informational Text in the Early Childhood Classroom." Chap. 8 in *Best Practices in Early Literacy Instruction,* eds. D.M. Barone & M.H. Mallette, 135–52. New York: Guilford.

Nancy Stockall
and Lindsay R.
Dennis

The Daily Dozen: Strategies for Enhancing Social Communication of Infants With Language Delays

Addie was born with cerebral palsy due to complications during birth. Because Addie is unable to swallow, she receives nutrition through a feeding tube. Addie's mom, Katie, who is a kindergarten teacher, is well aware of the risks of later language delays that might occur with Addie. She sought the advice of specialists to help enroll Addie in an early intervention program. Addie's participation in the program allowed Katie to return to work. Now she wants to know what she can do regularly to increase Addie's responsiveness to her and her husband during the family's time together.

Approximately 289,000 children from birth to age 3 are affected by a disability (US Census Bureau 2012). Developmental challenges may include severe, chronic disabilities that can begin at birth and last a lifetime. Delayed speech and language are the most common types of developmental delays among infants and toddlers (Rosenberg, Zhang, & Robinson 2008; Tomasello, Manning, & Dulmus 2010). Many such children are at risk for later language and literacy problems. To complicate matters, little research exists on the development and evaluation of prelinguistic teaching strategies for infants with developmental delays. However, some researchers (Fey et al. 2006) have

naeyc® 2, 3

found that early infant intervention in social communication at the prelinguistic stage holds promise for young children's later language success. But what exactly is prelinguistic communication?

Prelinguistic simply means before language, and it involves verbal and nonverbal communication. Parents and teachers can help infants develop these communication skills as they attend to the child's sounds, imitations, and responses to communication (Birckmayer, Kennedy, & Stonehouse 2010). A mother leans over the crib and smiles at her infant, cooing in a soft voice. In response, the infant smiles and kicks her feet in the air. Such interactions are early forms of communication and are the essential building blocks that support later complex language. It is important to note that many early prelinguistic forms of communication are unintentional. With repeated occurrences, these early forms of movement and vocalization transform into intentional communication, which typically occurs at about 9 months. But for infants with developmental delays, the move from unintentional to intentional communicative interaction often extends beyond 9 months.

The responsibility to engage infants in social communicative interactions lies most often with their primary caregivers. However, an extended stage of early communication places caregivers in the labor-intensive role of keeping up both sides of the interaction, sometimes referred to as *one-directional speech*. Sustaining the interaction in this way can become difficult, which means caregivers may become less responsive to an infant with developmental delays (Stephenson & Dowrick 2005; Warren & Brady 2007). Understanding the value and benefits of communicative interaction can encourage caregivers to consciously promote and sustain the interaction long after the novelty wears off. Families and teachers play an important role in the development of language and attention, and their ability to respond to children's communicative gestures and behaviors contributes to both social-emotional and linguistic development (Gartstein, Crawford, & Robertson 2008).

Nancy Stockall, PhD, is an associate professor at Sam Houston State University in Huntsville, Texas. She has published extensively in the field of special education, with a focus on semiotics and inclusion. Her research has been published nationally and internationally.

Lindsay R. Dennis, PhD, is an assistant professor of early childhood education at Sam Houston State University. Lindsay has worked in a variety of roles in support of children with disabilities and their families.

The Daily Dozen

We describe in this article a series of early language strategies that can help ease the strain of one-way communication with infants who might be slow to respond during social interactions. While these strategies are developmentally appropriate for all infants, they are especially critical when working with infants who have developmental delays. Infants with developmental delays may display several symptoms of delayed language development. Such symptoms include few vocalizations, communicative gestures, or spontaneous imitations and a reduced rate of nonverbal communication (Paul 2006; Ellis & Thal 2008). These strategies—we call them the Daily Dozen—may help alleviate these potential problems.

1. Establish a caring relationship

In a caring relationship, the caregiver is affectionate and responsive to the child's needs. One sign of affectionate behavior is positioning the infant to face the caregiver. Eye contact evolves from looking at the infant, and playful responsive behaviors involve singing or cooing to the infant and touching, kissing, and smiling at the infant. These types of behaviors emphasize emotional support and communicate the caregiver's interest and acceptance (Landry, Smith, & Swank 2006). Infants are likely to respond when they feel cared for and safe. Creating a safe environment and warm relationship with the infant supports a two-way interaction between the caregiver and child, while also inviting the infant to attempt and sustain a connection with the caregiver.

Infants with developmental delays may display several symptoms of delayed language development.

2. Take turns during interactions

Research suggests that children are likely to demonstrate more cooperative behavior when they share control with the caregiver and there is a sense of give-and-take between them (Landry, Smith, & Swank 2006). Whether verbal or nonverbal, give-and-take games help sustain caregiver–infant interactions. Smiling at the infant and waiting for a response, such as sharing your eye gaze, can be a kind of turn taking. For example, when Katie smiles and coos at Addie, Addie moves her arm in response and Katie repeats the process. Katie is patient with Addie, as sometimes it takes Addie a few seconds to respond to Katie's initiation. However, it is not just the wait time that Katie recognizes as important. Katie expects Addie to attempt a response and expresses that expectation through her facial expressions and the excitement in her voice.

3. Respond to the infant's nonverbal communication

It is important to remember that nonverbal imitations and gestures—motor imitation and vocal imitation—are early forms of language development. For infants with developmental delays involving muscle tone and strength, caregivers can use hand-over-hand guidance. For example, Katie waves to Addie and says "bye-bye." Then, taking Addie's left arm, she gently shakes Addie's hand, imitating the wave, and she again says "bye-bye." By modeling for Addie and then imitating the actions, Katie helps Addie learn that our bodies can convey messages just as our voices do. Katie also imitates Addie's vocalizations and models them for her. Research indicates that vocal imitations can influence later social interactions and scaffold language learning (Brady et al. 2004; Gros-Louis et al. 2006).

4. Use information talk

When a teacher talks with an infant about the actions she is performing, it enhances receptive vocabulary—words the child recognizes and understands. During routine activities such as diapering and changing an infant's clothing, the caregiver can talk about the actions taking place. Using consistent names for objects and events, as well as using talk and songs to make routines more predictable, is a great way to familiarize the child with his environment (Cho & Palmer 2008). Commenting on the activities provides the infant with opportunities to hear language and relate it to his environment, and it provides a context in which to make connections between words and actions. When Katie changes Addie's shirt, she comments on the choice of color and shows the shirt to Addie: "Here is the red shirt, Addie. We put one arm through the sleeve and then the other arm. Now it's time to push the snaps. Snap, snap, snap. All done. Now we are ready to go!"

5. Use a rich and varied vocabulary

Telling an infant what you are doing during caregiving routines is an important step in fostering communication. Describing your actions with rich language helps an infant understand and anticipate what is coming next (Kovach & Da Ros-Voseles 2011). Katie uses a wide variety of vocabulary with Addie, including simple nouns and action words, during daily routines such as bathing. Names of body parts and actions work well because they don't involve objects that the infant may not be able to hold. Katie uses bath time to play with Addie, saying, "We wash your toes and your feet . . . your arms and your hands and your belly! Splash, splash, splash goes the water . . . on your hands, on your feet, on your belly!"

> **Telling an infant what you are doing during caregiving routines is an important step in fostering communication.**

6. Use "motherese"

Infants prefer certain types of sounds that might also help them in learning language. For example, they often prefer speech that has a higher register, a variable pitch, and simpler, repetitive content (Falk 2004). The singsong structure of baby talk is one such type of speech often called *motherese*. As Katie bathes Addie, she glides the pitch of her voice up and down on the words *toes, feet, hands*, and *belly*. The intonation of these words emphasize the new information for Addie.

7. Draw the infant's attention

Pointing, gestures, touch, and mutual eye gaze all combine to make a rich context of interaction. Placing the child in a comfortable seating position provides a wide perspective of her environment (Brady et al. 2004) and also aids in promoting *joint attention*—the ability to coordinate attention between another person and some object. Joint attention is a significant predictor of later language development (Tomasello, Carpenter, & Liszkowski 2007). Katie can use a gentle touch to signal and/ or ask for Addie's participation in an interaction. She can also show Addie the object she wants her to attend to, thereby acknowledging that she wants Addie to engage with her and the object (Kovach & Da Ros-Voseles 2011).

8. Use meaningful talk that describes concepts

Children develop simple concepts—such as understanding the difference between up and down, or that red and blue are both colors—with help from adults. Other simple concepts describe positions in space (*above, below, over, under*) or physical condition (*wet, dry, smooth, rough*). When engaging in routine activities such as bathing, Katie washes Addie, saying, "The water is wet. Ohhh, all wet. Your arm is wet. Wet, wet, wet. Now we need to dry your arm." (See "Simple Concepts," p. 8.)

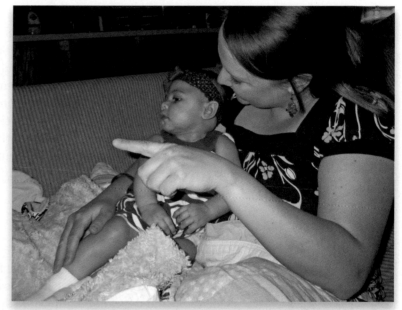

9. Use infant-directed speech

Infant-directed speech involves speaking in short sentences, repeating words frequently, and using parts of sentences rather than complete ones. It also involves raising and lowering language tones to sustain interaction. Infant-directed speech requires the caregiver to follow an infant's lead. When an infant coos or babbles, the caregiver can repeat the sounds and add more to what the infant initiates. Imitating the infant's initiations of sounds can increase the frequency of the turn taking, which can be a vehicle for later social interaction that is developmentally appropriate. Katie could also include her observation of Addie's response in her next message. For example, if Katie is talking about putting Addie's sock on and Addie raises her leg, Katie could say, "Addie, it looks like you want to help me put your sock on!"

10. Ask questions and use wait time

Questions are important in modeling the intonations of language. Asking simple questions such as "How big are you?" and answering "Soooo big" while raising an infant's arms are playful interactions that keep the child engaged. Waiting for the infant's response to the question creates an expectation of response, so that the infant can take a turn verbally with cooing noises or with motor responses such as kicking her feet. Asking questions allows you to experience a rich dialogue with an infant, even if you feel like you are doing all of the talking! By asking questions, waiting, and perhaps even providing a response when necessary, Katie is actually making interactions with Addie a bit easier and encouraging her participation in future exchanges.

Simple Concepts			
through	under	over	into
red	blue	green	purple
faster	slower	slowest	
soft	smooth	rough	
sweet	bitter	sour	
change	same	different	
happy	sad	worried	
before	after	in	out
high	low	slow	fast
below	above	black	white
wet	dry	solid	liquid

11. Listen with your eyes

Open your eyes wide when an infant responds. Look surprised and express joy in your play interactions. Joint attention to objects is enhanced when caregivers use expressive eye gaze. Some research indicates that infants prefer to look at the most expressive parts of the face, which includes the eyes and mouth (Lewkowicz & Hansen-Tift 2012). In our examples, Katie widens her eyes and smiles so that Addie stays attuned to the interaction.

12. Use social routines

Social routines include bathing, feeding, diapering, and playtime. Songs and finger plays are especially suited to playtime interaction. When playing games such as peeka-boo, remember that it may be necessary to take two turns first and then wait for the infant's response. A response can be verbal or nonverbal; therefore, when Addie kicks her feet in the air and moves her head toward the speaker, it signals a response. So look carefully at the infant's motor movements, and respond to her gurgles and coos. Repeated social encounters can help foster and grow the relationship between Katie and Addie, and ultimately enhance Addie's overall development.

Conclusion

Several short periods of play are sometimes more powerful than long, intense play sessions.

The definition of play includes doing something that is joyful and free flowing. Thus, interactions that take place should be fun for the caregiver as well as the infant. The overall goal of the interactions is to make the exchanges between caregiver and infant mutually pleasurable and developmentally appropriate. If it feels too much like work, it's best to take a break and return to the play at another time. The important thing is to remember that several short periods of play are sometimes more powerful than long, intense play sessions. Although developmental disabilities can be chronic, early intervention focused on prelinguistic skills holds promise for improving early language learning. Embedding prelinguistic skills in everyday play interactions can maximize the effect of these intervention strategies. In summary, caregivers can introduce and increase interactions that include attention and engagement. They may use intentional and reciprocal gestures and cues, vocal/verbal turn taking, elaboration of emotional responsiveness, and mutually pleasurable exchanges (Brady et al. 2004). The Daily Dozen are strategies that help to meet all of these prelinguistic developmental goals.

References

Birckmayer, J., A. Kennedy, & A. Stonehouse. 2010. "Sharing Spoken Language: Sounds, Conversations, and Told Stories." *Young Children* 65 (1): 34–39.

Brady, N., J. Marquis, K. Fleming, & L. McLean. 2004. "Prelinguistic Predictors of Language Growth in Children With Developmental Disabilities." *Journal of Speech, Language, and Hearing Research* 47 (3): 663–77.

Cho, H.-J., & S.B. Palmer. 2008. "Fostering Self-Determination in Infants and Toddlers With Visual Impairments or Blindness." *Young Exceptional Children* 11 (4): 26–34.

Ellis, E.M., & D.J. Thal. 2008. "Early Language Delay and Risk for Language Impairment." *Perspectives on Language Learning and Education* 15 (3): 93–100. http://div1perspectives.asha.org/content/15/3/93.full.pdf.

Falk, D. 2004. "Prelinguistic Evolution in Hominin Mothers and Babies: For Cryin' Out Loud!" *Behavioral and Brain Sciences* 27 (4): 461–2.

Fey, M.E., S.F. Warren, N. Brady, L.H. Finestack, S.L. Bredin-Oja, M. Fairchild, S. Sokol, & P.J. Yoder. 2006. "Early Effects of Responsivity Education/Prelinguistic Milieu Teaching for Children With Developmental Delays and Their Parents." *Journal of Speech, Language, and Hearing Research* 49 (3): 526–47.

Gartstein, M.A., J. Crawford, & C.D. Robertson. 2008. "Early Markers of Language and Attention: Mutual Contributions and the Impact of Parent-Infant Interactions." *Child Psychiatry and Human Development* 39 (1): 9–26.

Gros-Louis, J., M.J. West, M.H. Goldstein, & A.P. King. 2006. "Mothers Provide Differential Feedback to Infants' Prelinguistic Sounds." *International Journal of Behavioral Development* 30 (6): 509–16. http://babylab.psych.cornell.edu/wp-content/uploads/2009/04/groslouisgoldsteinijbd2006.pdf.

Kovach, B., & D. Da Ros-Voseles. 2011. "Communicating With Babies." *Young Children* 66 (2): 48–50.

Landry, S.H., K.E. Smith, & P.R. Swank. 2006. "Responsive Parenting: Establishing Early Foundations for Social, Communication, and Independent Problem-Solving Skills." *Developmental Psychology* 42 (4): 627–42. www.psy.miami.edu/faculty/dmessinger/c_c/rsrcs/rdgs/intervention/landrysmithswank2006.dp.pdf.

Lewkowicz, D.J., & A.M Hansen-Tift. 2012. "Infants Deploy Selective Attention to the Mouth of a Talking Face When Learning Speech." *Proceedings of the National Academy of Sciences of the United States of America,* 109 (5): 1431–1436. doi: 10.1073/pnas.1114783109.

Paul, R. 2006. *Language Disorders From Infancy Through Adolescence: Assessment and Intervention.* 3rd ed. St. Louis: Mosby.

Rosenberg, S.A., D. Zhang, & C.C. Robinson. 2008. "Prevalence of Developmental Delays and Participation in Early Intervention Services for Young Children." *Pediatrics* 121 (6): e1503–e1509. http://pediatrics.aap publications.org/content/121/6/e1503.full.pdf.

Stephenson, J., & M. Dowrick. 2005. "Parents' Perspectives on the Communication Skills of Their Children With Severe Disabilities." *Journal of Intellectual and Developmental Disability* 30 (2): 75–85.

Tomasello, M., M. Carpenter, & U. Liszkowski. 2007. "A New Look at Infant Pointing." *Child Development* 78 (3): 705–22. wwwstaff.eva.mpg.de/~tomas/pdf/Liszkowski_ChildDevlp_07.pdf.

Tomasello, N.M., A.R. Manning, & C.N. Dulmus. 2010. "Family-Centered Early Intervention for Infants and Toddlers With Disabilities." *Journal of Family Social Work* 13 (2): 163–72.

US Census Bureau. 2012. "Americans With Disabilities: 2010." www.census.gov/prod/2012pubs/p70-131.pdf.

Warren, S.F., & N.C. Brady. 2007. "The Role of Maternal Responsivity in the Development of Children With Intellectual Disabilities." *Mental Retardation and Developmental Disabilities Research Reviews* 13 (4): 330–8. http://olms.cte.jhu.edu/olms/data/resource/6174/Maternal%20Responsiveness%20and%20Intellectual%20Disability.pdf.

Nikki Darling-Kuria

What Do We Mean by Reading Readiness?

For the last several days, Janet has been anxious about her upcoming parent–teacher conference with Sam, 18-month-old Abby's father. Sam recently brought in alphabet flash cards because he wants Abby to learn to read. Janet completely understands Sam's desire to support his daughter's early language skills, but she is not comfortable with the method or the timing.

Janet brings her concerns to the director, Maria. "How can I help Sam understand that before Abby can read, she needs to have the strong foundational skills that come before letter recognition? You know we work on those skills every day. We tell stories, we talk to the children in ways that introduce them to new words and more complex use of language, and we read aloud from books and printed pages so they get the connection between words on a page and spoken language. Our training has taught us that flash cards for children so young are not effective in building toddlers' language skills. Their brains are not ready for rote memorization. But how do I say that to Sam so I support his interest without sounding critical?"

Maria understands the dilemma. She has been feeling the same pressure from other parents at the center. She says, "Have you asked Sam why he wants Abby to learn her ABCs now? Maybe the conference can be a time for you to hear about his hopes and goals for Abby. Then you can connect to those goals and share what you know about early language and literacy development. You can help him see that you and he are partners in supporting

Abby's language learning. One resource you could share with him is the new parent guide the state just published, the one that goes along with the state infant and toddler early learning guidelines you use in the toddler room."

Janet reads the parent guide and decides to begin the conference by asking about Sam's goals and expectations for Abby, as Maria suggested. It crosses her mind that Sam is probably using the best technique he knows of with the flash cards. If he is interested in discussing early language development and understanding how to support it, she will share the guide and explain the practices she uses with the children and connect those to emerging language skills.

Some families, wanting what is best for their children, believe that being able to read as early as possible is the best predictor of academic success later. After all, there is a constant bombardment of product advertisements promising that *any* child *any* age can become the next Einstein if the right combination of expensive toys and DVDs are purchased. It's easy to get caught up in the promises that new, better products will make smarter children. No wonder Janet and Sam have different ideas about what will work best!

Janet needs Sam's help in understanding his perspective, and Sam needs help in interpreting his observations about Abby's emerging language skills. Janet wants to establish a partnership with Sam that will benefit Abby's development. Her plan is to listen to and respond to Sam and share her knowledge about early development with him so that they can come to an agreement about what each can do to support Abby's emerging language skills.

Janet reflected on a recent infant brain development workshop she had attended to help her identify some talking points for the conference with Sam. Janet had learned that memorizing is often mistaken as learning. In fact, rote memorization is a lower level skill compared to skills developed through complex language use, which emerges in the context of meaningful relationships that motivate communication of thoughts and feelings (Hirsh-Pasek, Golinkoff, & Eyer 2003; Golinkoff & Hirsh-Pasek 2012). She knows that a great way to encourage Abby to talk is to pay attention to her and to what she is doing, making comments that connect to her experience. For example:

> "Abby, I see you ate all your chicken. Chicken is good for you and will help you grow big and STRONG [*arms out, flexing muscles*]!"

Janet plans to suggest that she and Abby's father both can keep this narration running throughout the day. They can describe a variety of emotions, like surprise, excitement, or sadness, as appropriate. Working together, they can give Abby the context she needs to make sense of all the new words she hears. For example, Sam can repeat the words Abby uses or use words in place of her gestures.

> Abby points to the cracker box and says "cra."
>
> Sam asks, "Would Abby like some crackers [*handing Abby the crackers*]? Are these the crackers that Abby wants?"

Sam can help give Abby her words until she is ready to do it herself, by modeling a rich vocabulary in the context of their everyday lives.

Nikki Darling-Kuria, MA, has worked in the field of early childhood care and education for over 18 years. She is a senior writer/training specialist at ZERO TO THREE.

Ways Teachers Can Increase Reading Readiness

Engage in Self-Reflection

- What are your beliefs about helping children become good communicators and readers?

- How do you go about building partnerships with families? Why is this important?

- What are some of the ways you share your practices with families? What are some early literacy and communication strategies you learned from families?

Put Ideas Into Action

- Develop some conversation starters that demonstrate your interest in partnering with families.

- Research your state's infant and toddler early learning guidelines. If your state doesn't have infant and toddler early learning guidelines, then use *Healthy Beginnings: Supporting Development and Learning From Birth Through Three Years of Age* (MSDE & Johns Hopkins University 2010), which you can access online at http://cte.jhu.edu/onlinecourses/HealthyBeginnings/HBFINAL.pdf.

- Create a book about the child's day that families can share at home with their child. Ask families to create a book about their child's day at home that you can share in your program.

- Create some talking points that share your knowledge about supporting emergent literacy in very young children. Practice with a colleague or mentor ways you might begin the conversations. For example:

  "Sam, I know how deeply you care about Abby's development. You really spend a lot of time with her in activities that you both enjoy. I appreciate the books you have brought in to share with the class, and I will use them. If you have any favorite rhyming songs that you sing at home, I would love to hear about them. I think that as we both continue to enjoy talking to Abby and reading and singing with her, she naturally will start talking more and learn more words. You will be amazed how quickly that happens. She will be eager and excited to learn to read when she's a little older."

The infant and toddler early learning guidelines, which explain what infants know and can do at various stages, provide Janet with further information to share about how toddlers develop and learn. Here is a sample of what she read about language and literacy for 18-month-olds. Children between the ages of 18 and 24 months are starting to "recognize and react to the sounds of language" (MSDE & Johns Hopkins University 2010, 21). That is why toddlers start paying attention to rhymes in songs and identifying sounds different animals make. Recognizing that a cow says "moo" and a dog says "ruff, ruff" is learning in context.

Another guideline states that children 18 to 24 months "begin to develop imitative reading"; for example, a child "might fill in words in a familiar text" (MSDE & Johns Hopkins University 2010, 21). Janet has noticed, and will share with Sam, that Abby finishes the phrases in a familiar book that is read to her. This is very exciting and shows that

Abby's language capacities are developing as expected for a child her age. Such seemingly simple activities build connections in Abby's brain and help her develop the skills she will need to communicate and help her when she is ready to read.

After deciding on an approach that will establish her respect for Sam's concerns and reflect her own understanding of infant language development, Janet felt better prepared for their conference. She was looking forward to hearing Sam's thoughts and sharing her learning. She was confident that together she and Sam could come up with realistic goals for Abby that centered on Abby's developing early reading skills that would last a lifetime.

References

Golinkoff, R.M., & K. Hirsh-Pasek. 2012. "Methods for Studying Language in Infants: Back to the Future." Chap. 5 in *Research Methods in Child Language: A Practical Guide*, ed. E. Hoff, 60–77. NY: Wiley-Blackwell.

Hirsh-Pasek, K., R.M. Golinkoff, & D. Eyer. 2003. *Einstein Never Used Flash Cards: How Our Children Really Learn— And Why They Need to Play More and Memorize Less.* Emmaus, PA: Rodale.

MSDE (Maryland State Department of Education) & Johns Hopkins University Center for Technology in Education. 2010. *Healthy Beginnings: Supporting Development and Learning From Birth Through Three Years of Age.* http://cte.jhu.edu/onlinecourses/HealthyBeginnings/ HBFINAL.pdf.

Resource

Gopnik, A. n.d. "Creating Healthy Connections: Nurturing Brain Development From Birth to Three." Podcast. 21 min. www.zerotothree.org/about-us/funded-projects/parenting-resources/podcast/creating-healthy-connections.html.

Molly F. Collins

Sagacious, Sophisticated, and Sedulous: The Importance of Discussing 50-Cent Words With Preschoolers

Ateacher once told me, "Don't use a 50-cent word when a 5-cent word will do."

While current expression of such sentiments might differ, we commonly follow this practice in many early childhood classrooms. Adults often use simple words instead of complex words when talking to young children. Reasons vary from teachers' beliefs that young children cannot understand sophisticated vocabulary because they are too young or have limited language skills, to teachers'

unfamiliarity with complex words or with strategies for supporting vocabulary. As a consequence, sophisticated vocabulary learning is thwarted and opportunities to nurture children's curiosity about words go unrealized. In this article, I show how to fortify the vocabulary knowledge of soon-to-be readers with *sophisticated vocabulary*—words that are high level, communicate subtleties in detail, and are less common in everyday parlance (sometimes called *rare words*).

naeyc® 2, 3

Early Language Foundations for Reading Development

Research on the early foundations of reading distinguishes two categories of skills—one related to word recognition and the other related to comprehension. Print knowledge, beginning writing skills, and phonological awareness have been grouped together as *word recognition* skills because they help children decode text. These *code-related* skills account for most of a child's success in word recognition, the major task of beginning reading. Vocabulary, syntactic and discourse skills, and background knowledge have been grouped together as *oral language* or *comprehension* skills (Storch & Whitehurst 2002; Sénéchal, Ouellette, & Rodney 2006). Developed in preschool, oral language skills predict later reading comprehension beyond the contribution made by word recognition skills in the early grades (NICHD Early Child Care Research Network 2005).

Vocabulary is highly sensitive to early adult input and critical to preventing later reading comprehension difficulties (Dickinson et al. 2003). Also, vocabulary is causally related to comprehension—that is, it helps reading comprehension (Dickinson et al. 2003)—and it is highly correlated with the rate of learning new words (Rowe, Raudenbush, & Goldin-Meadow 2012). Thus, a meager beginning vocabulary slows the rate of vocabulary learning, which compromises reading comprehension.

Two widely examined contexts for early language development are conversations and storybook reading. Pan and colleagues (2005) found that exposure to unfamiliar words in mothers' talk with children is related to children's vocabulary growth. Research on teachers' talk at mealtimes shows a positive relationship between conversations and preschoolers' vocabulary development (Cote 2001). Robust word learning has been found extensively in story reading contexts (De Temple & Snow 2003).

While numerous studies have examined vocabulary acquisition, most focus on common words—that is, high-frequency vocabulary. A few studies examine children's acquisition of sophisticated, or low-frequency, vocabulary. Dickinson and Porche (2011) find that preschool teachers' use of complex vocabulary during play contributes to children's reading comprehension in fourth grade. Research shows that among preschoolers in families with low incomes, there is a positive relationship between the amount of exposure to sophisticated words and supportive explanations during conversations with parents and children's later vocabulary (Weizman & Snow 2001). In storybook reading contexts, Beck and McKeown (2007) find that kindergartners and first-graders from families with low incomes learn sophisticated words from robust instruction during read-alouds. Preschoolers who hear rich explanations of sophisticated words learn significantly more words than children who do not (Collins 2010). These studies provide compelling evidence for the benefits of teaching sophisticated vocabulary to children in preschool through first grade, and they describe useful strategies and contexts for supporting this development.

Benefits of Talking About 50-Cent Words With Young Children

Opportunities for initiating conversations about rare words can come from storybook reading experiences. Discussing words with children prompts their active involvement and provides teachers with information about children's evolving lexicons. In fact,

> Preschoolers who hear rich explanations of sophisticated words learn significantly more words than children who do not.

Molly F. Collins, EdD, is a lecturer in the Department of Teaching and Learning at Peabody College, Vanderbilt University, in Nashville. Molly's teaching and research focus on children's vocabulary acquisition and story comprehension, and on instructional quality in preschool. She is the coauthor with Judith A. Schickedanz of the 2012 NAEYC book *So Much More Than the ABCs*.

conversations about words provide more information about a child's developing vocabulary knowledge than we can learn from tests or observations of children's word use. Benefits of conversations about sophisticated vocabulary include the following, learned from talking with preschoolers.

They expose children to new words and new concepts. Talking about unusual (i.e., low-frequency) vocabulary exposes children to new words in a context that is visually and verbally supportive. The following illustrates how a teacher exposed children to the word *unruly* in the course of discussing the text in *Henry's Happy Birthday,* by Holly Keller.

> **Ms. Doran:** *Unruly* means hard to control. It was hard for Henry to make his hair do what he wanted it to do—stay down. Your hair might be unruly when you wake up in the morning.
>
> **Jason:** Yeah, my mom's hair is messy.
>
> **Ms. Doran:** When she first wakes up?
>
> **Jason:** Yeah, all over, like this *(hands circling head)*.
>
> **Ms. Doran:** It sounds like her hair is unruly, too. Hard to control.

Ms. Doran's use of *unruly* in a short discussion of Henry's appearance exposes children to a sophisticated word whose concept they can easily understand.

They clarify differences in meaning between new words and known concepts. Talking about words offers teachers opportunities to clarify nuances in word meanings. The following conversation during a reading of Lindsay Barrett George's *In the Woods: Who's Been Here?* shows how talking about sophisticated vocabulary helps adults understand what children pay attention to in definitions and how adults can provide clarification to help children understand word meanings.

> **Mr. Myers:** When it *(pointing to butterfly)* was inside, its wings were together, but once it got out, it could splay, or spread out, its wings.
>
> **Aquala:** Ya!
>
> **Mr. Myers:** *Splay* means to spread out.
>
> **Aquala:** Yeah, like peanut butter. Like spread with a knife.
>
> **Mr. Myers:** Yes, but the peanut butter doesn't really get splayed because it doesn't have parts. *Splay* means to spread something that has parts. You have body parts that you can splay. You can splay your arms, legs. And spread out all over like this *(gestures)*.
>
> **Aquala:** *(pointing to stomach)* Can't splay this!
>
> **Mr. Myers:** No, you can't splay your stomach. You can't splay your tongue. So you can only splay things that have parts to spread out.
>
> **Aquala:** *(spreading arms apart)* This splay?
>
> **Mr. Myers:** Yes, you are splaying your arms.
>
> **Aquala:** *(to another child)* And you are splaying your whole body.

This conversation included general information about *splay*'s meaning. When the child applied a literal understanding of *spread,* however, the adult clarified that splaying requires parts and differs from spreading a substance.

They deepen meanings of partially known words. Sometimes children's knowledge about words is limited to only one derivation, to a single context, or to examples, not meanings. Discussion provides opportunities to deepen children's knowledge of words, as follows in a conversation during a reading of William T. George's *Box Turtle at Long Pond.*

> **Ms. Fradon:** A *predator* is an animal that eats other animals.
>
> **Garth:** Like a tiger. Like a tiger eats an antelope.
>
> **Ms. Fradon:** Yes.
>
> **Garth:** Because *(pointing to raccoon)* they eat turtles.
>
> **Ms. Fradon:** So, a raccoon is a predator of?
>
> **Garth:** Of the ... of the *(pointing to turtle)*
>
> **Ms. Fradon:** Box turtle. Exactly.
>
> **Caritina:** *(pointing to raccoon)* Yep, that's a predator.

This conversation provided information about the characteristics of a *predator,* a word for which Garth has partial knowledge through examples (tiger). Garth later indicated an understanding of the meaning of *predator* by stating "Because they eat turtles." He seemed to use the basic meaning of *predator* to judge that the raccoon qualifies. Still using examples, Caritina agreed: "Yep, that's a predator." The conversation exemplifies application of the new information to animals in the book, deepening the children's knowledge of predator exemplars.

They repair misunderstandings. Talking about sophisticated words with preschoolers enables adults to repair children's initial misunderstandings of new words, especially if children have missed important distinctions in meaning, have not heard the word precisely, or have misapplied their existing knowledge or *metalinguistic information*—knowledge about language (e.g., knowing that words ending in *-ing* are probably actions). The following example is from a conversation about illustrations of *bunting* during a reading of *Henry's Happy Birthday.*

> **Mr. Chua:** Do you know what bunting is?
>
> **Antoine:** Uh-uh [no].
>
> **Mr. Chua:** *(to Val)* Do you know?
>
> **Val:** Uh-huh [yes]. It's putting up things.
>
> **Mr. Chua:** Not quite. Bunting is a decoration.
>
> **Val:** Uh-huh.

Mr. Chua: And it's cloth or paper that is hung up to make parties look pretty. It is a decoration—something pretty. Sometimes grown-ups put bunting up to decorate a room or even the outside of a building.

Val's first response indicates that she thinks the word *bunting* is a verb. The *-ing* ending seems to indicate to her that the word labels some action: "putting things up." Mr. Chua then clarifies that *bunting* is a noun, something that is put up, not the action of hanging something. When a teacher models accurate use of misunderstood information in the explanation, children learn exactly why the initial meaning is problematic.

They prime children to value words and increase their knowledge about word learning. Exposing children to uncommon words and their definitions can shape children's expectations to hear explanations and to wonder about word meanings. In the next example, a teacher reads Jim Arnosky's *Rabbits and Raindrops* and inserts a low-frequency word, *lawn,* which Ms. Krigstein had explained previously.

Ms. Krigstein: Mother rabbit hops out—jumps quickly—into the bright sunlight, onto the green grass, that green lawn. So mother rabbit is leading her babies on the green lawn.

Wallace: The green grass?

Ms. Krigstein: Yes, the green grass is the green lawn.

Modeling the belief that sophisticated words are interesting and important to know communicates to children that words are worthy of children's curiosity. Talking about unusual words provides benefits to children beyond simply hearing them or having rich definitions. When children learn sophisticated words through discussion, they might begin to realize that they sometimes misunderstand a meaning. Knowing this is a possibility, and that specific details are involved in distinguishing a sophisticated word, children seem to learn to check their understanding of key details in words' meanings. This child believes queries about words are welcome and that words in the story should make sense.

> Modeling the belief that sophisticated words are interesting and important communicates that words are worthy of children's curiosity.

Implications for Teaching

Teaching sophisticated vocabulary from storybook reading and discussions of words requires that adults know the words and their variations across contexts. Helping children use words beyond the story-reading context requires expanding instruction, or "thinking outside the book."

Knowing What to Know

Children need to know the basic definition of a word in its most typical or general form. The basic meaning gives children a working understanding of the word's most common meaning and use (Stahl & Nagy 2006).

Knowing a word includes understanding how its meaning varies. This contributes to depth of word knowledge and requires exposures across several contexts. When the same word is used in different scenarios, it strengthens children's understandings of its meaning. An umbrella's fabric *repels* water. Magnets also *repel* one another when like poles are aligned. Bug spray *repels* insects. Although these ideas differ, all mean to "push away from" or "ward off." Exposure to the same word across settings can also teach differences in meaning. A shirt can have *crisp* folds. *Crisp* crackers break easily. Morning air can feel *crisp*. To know words means to learn variations. This requires early, continued exposure across contexts.

Knowing a word also means knowing its mechanics, such as its pronunciation, the slot it fills in a sentence (noun, verb, adjective, and so on), and the meaning of its parts (e.g., in *untidy,* the prefix *un* means *not*). Soon-to-be readers learn mechanics from adults' modeling. For example, a person can have many *interests*. *Interest* can be shown. Being *interested* differs from being *interesting*. Children have access to this type of knowledge about words when adults use words with them.

Thinking Outside the Book

Children's exposure to sophisticated vocabulary must extend beyond discussions about storybooks. Using the words deliberately with children throughout the day, such as in conversations and during activities, provides repeated exposure and helps develop meaning across contexts. For example, a teacher might explain the word *persevere* when it is first encountered in a storybook, use the word later in activities with children, and use it again during a conversation about young siblings (see "Using *Persevere* Across Multiple Contexts"). In these ways, sophisticated vocabulary relating to meaningful content is modeled and valued in children's vernacular.

Using *Persevere* Across Multiple Contexts

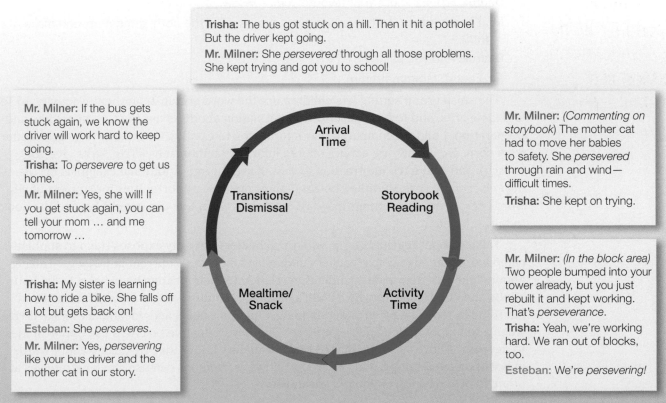

Trisha: The bus got stuck on a hill. Then it hit a pothole! But the driver kept going.
Mr. Milner: She *persevered* through all those problems. She kept trying and got you to school!

Mr. Milner: If the bus gets stuck again, we know the driver will work hard to keep going.
Trisha: To *persevere* to get us home.
Mr. Milner: Yes, she will! If you get stuck again, you can tell your mom ... and me tomorrow ...

Trisha: My sister is learning how to ride a bike. She falls off a lot but gets back on!
Esteban: She *perseveres*.
Mr. Milner: Yes, *persevering* like your bus driver and the mother cat in our story.

Mr. Milner: (*Commenting on storybook*) The mother cat had to move her babies to safety. She *persevered* through rain and wind—difficult times.
Trisha: She kept on trying.

Mr. Milner: (*In the block area*) Two people bumped into your tower already, but you just rebuilt it and kept working. That's *perseverance*.
Trisha: Yeah, we're working hard. We ran out of blocks, too.
Esteban: We're *persevering*!

Arrival Time — Storybook Reading — Activity Time — Mealtime/Snack — Transitions/Dismissal

Providing concrete examples of sophisticated vocabulary is another way to think outside the book. A teacher might show and label a sieve in a demonstration of washing berries. The teacher could give a definition of *sieve*—a wire mesh utensil—as well as information about its function: straining water from washed fruit. The sieve's features (e.g., handles, size and placement of holes) make it suitable for some types of food but not others. The teacher might use it with children, show examples of types of sieves, discuss different functions (e.g., sifting, ricing, puréeing), or show examples of sieves in different contexts, such as construction, mining, or archaeology. Finally, children can use sieves in cooking and in outdoor and water play activities.

Another way to think outside the book is to use words in conversations. Children need opportunities to produce new vocabulary in a variety of settings. Small groups—which are especially helpful for dual language learners and children who are introverted—help children produce words. Combined with hands-on examples, this small group setting fosters rich interaction and talk about *grits*.

Mr. Eacott: Did you want any grits?

Shareen: Grits give you energy.

Mr. Eacott: Yes, they give you energy.

Daaruk: But I don't like grits.

Mr. Eacott: Grits? But grits are made out of corn.

Daaruk: Grits? Grits?

Mr. Eacott: Mm-hm. Made out of corn. You don't like corn? Don't you like corn? I like corn.

Daaruk: At least that's your favorite color—yellow.

Mr. Eacott: It sure is. They just take out the inside of the corn, grind it up, and make grits.

Daaruk: And you eat it?

Mr. Eacott: Mmmm-hmmm.

The small group setting lets children use the word *grits* in an authentic activity, to see and taste grits, and to hear descriptive information about its features, composition, and preparation. Children compared new information to existing knowledge (e.g., grits come from corn, are yellow, are eaten), offered information themselves (e.g., grits give you energy), and evaluated information in view of skepticism. Additional examples in "Using *Persevere* Across Multiple Contexts" show multiple opportunities for support of new words across several settings in a day. Moreover, word talk can extend beyond the book to talk at home.

Talking about unusual words with preschoolers not only exposes them to sophisticated words but also helps teachers understand children's current knowledge. Talking about children's new understandings in relation to their existing knowledge helps both adults and children learn why a child's misunderstandings might be well founded and plausible in view of a naive understanding. Children's skills and vocabulary intake thrive when adult input is rich and responsive. Therefore, effective teachers use opportunities to develop children's sophisticated oral vocabulary knowledge by talking about words in books, conversations, and classroom activities. Families can use similar strategies at home to help develop children's vocabulary.

A Few Parting Words

Adults must be *sagacious* (wise) in providing exposure to, and support for, learning rare words in preschool. We must be *sophisticated* (complex) in our selection and consideration of worthy words and bathe children in supportive talk about these words. Finally, we must be *sedulous* (diligent) in preparation for teaching and using vocabulary across multiple contexts. If children start early to develop broad and deep oral repertoires, there is strong potential for their later reading comprehension to be robust. We can strengthen children's literacy development by exposing preschoolers to sophisticated vocabulary, by using it in multiple contexts, and by giving helpful information about a word's meaning through explanations and discussions. The 50-cent words are worth it.

References

Beck, I.L., & M.G. McKeown. 2007. "Increasing Young Low-Income Children's Oral Vocabulary Repertoires Through Rich and Focused Instruction." *The Elementary School Journal* 107 (3): 251–73.

Collins, M.F. 2010. "ELL Preschoolers' English Vocabulary Acquisition From Storybook Reading." *Early Childhood Research Quarterly* 25 (1): 84–97.

Cote, L.R. 2001. "Language Opportunities During Mealtimes in Preschool Classrooms." Chap. 9 in *Begining Literacy With Language: Young Children Learning at Home and School,* eds. D.K. Dickinson & P.O. Tabors, 205–22. Baltimore: Brookes.

De Temple, J., & C.E. Snow. 2003. "Learning Words From Books." Chap. 2 in *On Reading Books to Children: Teachers and Parents,* eds. A. van Kleeck, S.A. Stahl, & E.B. Bauer, 16–36. Mahwah, NJ: Erlbaum.

Dickinson, D.K., A. McCabe, L. Anastasopoulos, E.S. Peisner-Feinberg, & M.D. Poe. 2003. "The Comprehensive Language Approach to Early Literacy: The Interrelationships Among Vocabulary, Phonological Sensitivity, and Print Knowledge Among Preschool-Aged Children." *Journal of Educational Psychology* 95 (3): 465–81.

Dickinson, D.K., & M.V. Porche. 2011. "Relation Between Language Experiences in Preschool Classrooms and Children's Kindergarten and Fourth-Grade Language and Reading Abilities." *Child Development* 82 (3): 870–86.

NICHD Early Child Care Research Network. 2005. "Pathways to Reading: The Role of Oral Language in the Transition to Reading." *Developmental Psychology* 41 (2): 428–42.

Pan, B.A., M.L. Rowe, J.D. Singer, & C.E. Snow. 2005. "Maternal Correlates of Growth in Toddler Vocabulary Production in Low-Income Families." *Child Development* 76 (4): 763–82.

Rowe, M.L., S.W. Raudenbush, & S. Goldin-Meadow. 2012. "The Pace of Vocabulary Growth Helps Predict Later Vocabulary Skill." *Child Development* 83 (2): 508–25.

Sénéchal, M., G. Ouellette, & D. Rodney. 2006. "The Misunderstood Giant: On the Predictive Role of Early Vocabulary to Future Reading." Chap. 13 in *Handbook of Early Literacy Research, Volume 2,* eds. D.K. Dickinson & S.B. Neuman, 173–82. New York: Guilford.

Stahl, S.A., & W.E. Nagy. 2006. *Teaching Word Meanings.* Mahwah, NJ: Erlbaum.

Storch, S.A., & G.J. Whitehurst. 2002. "Oral Language and Code-Related Precursors to Reading: Evidence From a Longitudinal Structural Model." *Developmental Psychology* 38 (6): 934–47.

Weizman, Z.O., & C.E. Snow. 2001. "Lexical Input as Related to Children's Vocabulary Acquisition: Effects of Sophisticated Exposure and Support for Meaning." *Developmental Psychology* 37 (2): 265–79.

J. Michelle
Huffman and
Callie
Fortenberry

naeyc ® 2, 3

Helping Children Prepare for Writing: Developing Fine Motor Skills

On a crisp September morning during my first year teaching kindergarten, Mrs. Lucio and I [Michelle] meet to discuss her son's progress. I eagerly share that Mario is inquisitive, creative, and quite intelligent. His literacy skills are emerging rapidly. He can identify all upper- and lowercase letters, is phonemically aware, and recognizes many sight words. However, Mario has great difficulty writing his name.

Mrs. Lucio's frustration and confusion are evident. The family has provided Mario with pencils, paper, and hand-over-hand writing demonstrations. They have done all they know to do to help him master this skill. How can it be that this child is not able to write his name?

Early childhood is the most intensive period for the development of physical skills (NASPE 2012). Writing progress depends largely on the development of fine motor skills involving small muscle movements of the hand. Muscle development for writing is a comprehensive process that begins with movements of the whole arm and progresses toward very detailed fine motor control at the fingertips (Adolph 2008). Much like an amateur runner who cannot run a marathon without proper training, a child cannot master the art of conventional writing without the proper foundation of muscle development.

Young children need to participate in a variety of developmentally appropriate activities intentionally designed to promote fine motor control. Fine motor skills are difficult for preschoolers to master because the skills depend on muscular control, patience, judgment, and brain coordination (Carvell 2006). Children develop motor skills at different rates. It is important for teachers to encourage motor development with developmentally appropriate tasks that are achievable at any age and with any skill set (Bruni 2006).

Stages of Fine Motor Development

Just as there is a progression in gaining cognitive abilities, so too there is a sequence in developing muscles. Four stages of fine motor development set the stage for early writing success—whole arm, whole hand, pincher, and pincer coordination (Carvell 2006). Fine motor development begins with strengthening and refining the muscles of the whole arm. As young children participate in large arm-movement activities, such as painting a refrigerator box with paint rollers and water or tossing a beach ball into a laundry basket, they use their entire arm. This full arm movement is a precursor to muscle development of the hand.

Pouring water from one container to another and squeezing water from a turkey baster develop the muscles of the whole hand. Strengthening the hand muscles leads to the ability to coordinate the finer movements of the fingers. Children develop the pincher movements by pressing the thumb and index finger together. Clipping clothespins on a plastic cup, stringing beads, and tearing paper are activities that support this development.

Pincer control is the final stage of fine motor development. With other skills in place, children are now prepared to properly grasp markers, pencils, and other writing utensils as they engage in authentic writing activities. This coordination allows the thumb and the index and middle fingers to act as a tripod, supporting the writing utensil and enabling small, highly coordinated finger movements.

In the Classroom

As noted in the NAEYC Early Childhood Program Standards, teachers can give children multiple and varied opportunities to support their physical development. The daily routine, frequency of activities that foster fine motor development, and types of materials teachers provide all influence children's muscle development (NAEYC 2007). In "Activities That Promote Fine Motor Development" (p. 24), we suggest a number of easily implemented activities teachers can use that enhance young children's fine motor development.

J. Michelle Huffman, EdD, is assistant professor of education at Texas A&M University–Texarkana. Michelle has worked in the early childhood field for over 20 years. She currently teaches emergent literacy and early childhood courses.

Callie Fortenberry, EdD, is associate professor of education and reading at Texas A&M University–Texarkana. Callie teaches education and emergent literacy courses and works closely with preservice early childhood teachers.

Activities That Promote Fine Motor Development

These simple activities engage children in different levels of motor development in preparation for writing.

Muscle development	Activity and materials	Description
Whole arm	**Under-the-Table Art** Large sheet of drawing paper, tape, and crayons or chalk	Tape the paper to the underside of a table. Children lie on their backs under the table, extend the arm with crayon or chalk in hand, and draw on the paper.
	Ribbons and Rings Set of plastic bracelets and 12 inches of colored ribbon for each bracelet	Attach a ribbon to each bracelet using a simple slip-knot. Play music. Children wear or hold their bracelets and use their bracelet arms to make big circles, wave the ribbons high and low, and perform other creative movements.
	Stir It Up! Large pot, long wooden spoon, and pebbles	Put the dry ingredients and the spoon in the pot, and place it in the dramatic play area. Children stir the "soup" using a large circular arm motion.
Whole hand	**Sponge Squeeze** Small sponge, divided food dish, and water	Fill one side of the dish with water. Children transfer the water from side to side by dipping and squeezing the sponge.
	Lid Match Two baskets and a collection of plastic containers with matching lids (spice jars, margarine tubs, yogurt cups, shampoo containers, hand cream jars, and such)	Sort the containers and lids into separate baskets. Children match and attach the lids to the right containers.
	Sand Sifting Crank-style sifter, large bowl, and fine sand	Place the empty sifter in the bowl. Children use two hands to pour the sand into the sifter, then turn the crank handle to sift the sand into the bowl.
Pincher	**Button Drop** Four plastic containers with lids, and buttons	Cut a slit in each lid and label each container with a color. Children sort the buttons by color and drop them into the appropriate containers.
	Color Transfer Eyedroppers, muffin tin, food coloring, water, and a section of rubber bath mat backed with suction cups	Fill the muffin tin compartments with water of different colors. Children use the eyedroppers to transfer drops of colored water into each suction cup.
	Using Tongs Spring-handle metal tongs, sorting trays (ice cube trays, egg cartons, divided dishes, small containers), and items to sort (counting bears, acorns, buttons, pom-poms)	Show children how to use their thumb and middle and index fingers to manipulate the tongs. Children use the tongs to pick up the items and sort them into separate compartments or containers.
Pincer	**Capture the Cork!** Corks in a variety of sizes, a bowl of water, and tweezers	Put the corks in the bowl of water. Children use the tweezers to capture the floating corks.
	Locks and Keys A variety of small locks with keys	Close the locks. Children determine which keys work with which locks and unlock them.
	Clip It A variety of small barrettes, hair clips, and elastic bands; dolls with hair; brushes and combs; and a tray for materials	Children use the hair fasteners or elastic bands to divide the dolls' hair into small sections. Clips that fasten in different ways and small elastic bands support a range of motor skill levels.

Adapted with permission from Nell R. Carvell, *Language Enrichment Activities Program (LEAP)*, vol. 1 (Dallas, TX: Southern Methodist University, 2006).

Conclusion

Many kindergartners feel frustrated when they face the daunting task of conventional writing. In Mario's case, we identified the root of his writing difficulty—lack of motor development in his hands. We planned ways to support his developmental needs. Rather than asking Mario to write, we replaced paper and pencil tasks with developmentally appropriate experiences that helped him develop his fine motor skills.

When preschool teachers observe children, they have endless opportunities to gather information about each child (Copple & Bredekamp 2009). Throughout the day, perceptive teachers use their keen sense of observation to note how children use their arms, hands, and fingers. Responsive teachers can alleviate frustration and nurture emerging fine motor skills by providing materials and activities that support differentiated instruction for each stage of physical development. With intentional planning and preparation, classroom environments can build children's whole-arm, whole-hand, pincher, and pincer coordination in preparation for learning to write.

References

Adolph, K.E. 2008. "Motor and Physical Development: Locomotion." In *Encyclopedia of Infant and Early Childhood Development*, eds. M.M. Haith & J.B. Benson, 359–73. San Diego, CA: Academic Press.

Bruni, M. 2006. *Fine Motor Skills for Children With Down Syndrome: A Guide for Parents and Professionals.* Bethesda, MD: Woodbine House.

Carvell, N.R. 2006. *Language Enrichment Activities Program (LEAP),* vol. 1. Dallas, TX: Southern Methodist University.

Copple, C., & S. Bredekamp, eds. 2009. *Developmentally Appropriate Practice in Early Childhood Programs Serving Children From Birth Through Age 8.* 3rd ed. Washington, DC: NAEYC.

NAEYC. 2007. *NAEYC Early Childhood Program Standards and Accreditation Criteria: The Mark of Quality in Early Childhood Education.* Rev. ed. Washington DC: NAEYC.

NASPE (National Association for Sport and Physical Education) & AHA (American Heart Association). 2012. *2012 Shape of the Nation Report: Status of Physical Education in the USA.* Reston, VA: NASPE.

Barbara A. Marinak, Martha J. Strickland, and Jane Blakely Keat

Using Photo-Narration to Support the Language Development of All Learners

That was a cool picture when I got it [referring to his photograph of a cake]. It's got cake and it's a little disgusting.
—Matthew, Age 3

I loved my pictures.
—Nayla, Age 3

This article describes collaboration between three university professors and six preschool teachers who used photo-narration and the language experience approach (Labbo 2005; Lenters 2004; Stauffer 1970) to support the language development of young children.

The Language Experience Approach

For more than a century, educators have used children's personal experiences as a basis for language and literacy instruction (Huey [1908] 1968). The language experience approach (LEA) draws on the important link between experience and education; it extends the practice of scribing a child's discussion to using the child's narrative as the text for reading instruction (Lenters 2004). Using a child's stories, a teacher can engage the child in discussion about important text features as well as invite the child to reread and possibly revise the stories.

naeyc ® 2, 3

Research shows that LEA is a developmentally appropriate method for gathering the words of young children (Allen 1968; Clark & Moss 2011). With this method, children's language is a response to teachers' supportive questioning. This approach also demonstrates to children that anything that is said can be written, and anything that is written can be read or said.

LEA supports children's concept development and vocabulary growth while offering many opportunities for meaningful reading and writing. Important conversations with teachers and child-produced records (in our project, photos) can extend children's knowledge of the world around them while building a sense of classroom community (Nessel & Dixon 2008).

In this approach, children are actively involved in planning, experiencing, and responding to their scribed words. LEA can be used in any situation to clarify for children the link between oral language and print. The steps we took in this project are described in "Suggestions for Using the Language Experience Approach" (p. 29).

A Diverse School

This photo-narration project took place in a culturally and linguistically diverse preschool that also included children with special needs. The teachers were interested in learning how to better meet the needs of all the learners through an investigation of culturally responsive teaching. Each classroom included dual language learners. All families participated in the project, including 14 families representing nine countries and 15 languages. Teachers sent a letter to each family describing the project, which included all the children in the six classrooms.

It was this diversity that prompted the teachers to request assistance from us, three professors of education with expertise in literacy, early childhood, and educational psychology. After considering the preschool teachers' stated needs, we suggested that a yearlong project using photo-narration might help them make meaningful connections with all the children.

Photo-narration is a process in which a person takes photos and then describes the photos to another to illuminate his or her world for the listener (Clark-Ibáñez 2004). In this case, children described to their teachers the photographs they took.

The Project Begins

Teachers gave each child a disposable camera. To introduce the cameras to the children, our preschool colleagues devoted one circle time to teaching the children how to take photographs. The teachers read aloud a Big Book about visual perspective (*Look, Look, Look,* by Tana Hoban) and shared important photographs from their own lives (homes, children, pets, and so on). After discussing the photographs and learning how to use a camera, the children practiced pressing the button on a camera by taking turns with a small book titled *Diego and Click Take a Pic!,* by Lara Bergen. This children's book is in the shape of a camera and includes a square opening (viewfinder) and a red button to click so children can pretend to take a photo.

At the conclusion of circle time, each child received a take-home baggie containing a disposable camera and a second parent letter. In this letter, teachers reminded families

> Important conversations with teachers and child-produced records (in our project, photos) can extend children's knowledge of the world around them.

Barbara A. Marinak, PhD, is associate professor in the School of Education and Human Services at Mount St. Mary's University. Her research interests include reading engagement, intervention practices, and the use of informational text.

Martha J. Strickland, EdD, is associate professor of education in educational psychology at the Pennsylvania State University, Harrisburg. She has worked and taught internationally. Her research focus is on the impact of culture on learning.

Jane Blakely Keat, PhD, is associate professor and program coordinator of early childhood education at the Pennsylvania State University, Harrisburg. She has studied the potential of the communication dance between learner and teacher as a preschool teacher, professor, and researcher.

about the purpose of the camera activity and the importance of making sure that the children choose which items to photograph. The letter also included a list of suggested subjects children might wish to photograph—family members, possessions, rooms, pets, food, and so on.

We used disposable cameras instead of digital cameras for several reasons. First, we wanted the children to feel free to take the cameras anywhere to photograph their world. Second, given that the children took photographs for about a week, the cameras needed to be portable and replaceable in case of an accident. We encouraged the children to take photos of anything they wanted.

When the children returned the cameras, we professors had the film developed and placed the photos in small individual photo albums. The teachers then asked each child to "choose three photographs to talk about." They marked the photos with small stickers to help the children remember their selections. After the children chose three photos, the teachers had one-on-one conversations with each child to talk about the those pictures. These chats took place in a quiet hallway at a small table while we professors observed. A substitute teacher covered the classroom.

All the discussions took place in English; however, dual language learners used a variety of verbal and nonverbal techniques to communicate about their photos. For example, one child simply pointed to items within the photo and looked intently at the teacher. Other children labeled the subject(s) of the photo, and many children recounted what they were thinking about when they took the photo. Many described the photo and the context with elaborative descriptions. We digitally recorded the narrations and transcribed them (parents had consented to this).

Photo-narration is a process in which a person takes photos and then describes the photos to another to illuminate his or her world for the listener.

The children and their teachers revisited each of the three favorite photos three times over a period of approximately four months. Each time, the teacher and child created a new story, resulting in a total of nine stories for each child. True to the language experience approach, the teachers listened to each story and wrote down the children's words exactly.

Language Experience Story Examples

The preschool teacher began by asking the child about his or her photos. The teacher encouraged the child to talk about the subject in whatever manner was comfortable (standing, sitting, touching or holding the photos, and so on). The dialogue included several components. First, the child described the details of the photograph. Second, the child usually ascribed personal meaning to the contents of the photo. Third, the teacher listened intently to the child. And fourth, the teacher asked a few questions to invite the child to expand on the subject. As the child spoke, the teacher neatly printed the child's words on an index card. When the child was finished, the teacher and child reviewed the dictation and read it together. The teacher placed the index card in the photo album under the appropriate picture.

These stories and the photos that inspired them were important, and teachers treated them accordingly. This approach supported children's concept development and vocabulary growth, offering many opportunities for meaningful discussions and sharing. We took great care to protect the photo albums. Of course, the children eagerly talked about their photos with their teachers and classmates, but the albums were stored carefully at the end of each day.

The following are samples from the stories of the dual language learners over the course of four months. These examples reveal complex sentences, embedded questions, and rich descriptions.

> A child from Cambodia is looking at her photograph of an aquarium.
> **Story 1:** That's Crabby. Why did Daddy put Crabby in there? I'm glad it's not in my room.
> **Story 2:** That's Nibbles. He was born from the big goldfish. And there are two crabbies. It's my brother's room.
> **Story 3:** That's Little Nibbles. That's Goldie. I don't know that name, but it's a crab.

> A child from India is looking at a picture of herself holding a balloon.
> **Story 1:** This is me with my balloons from my birthday.
> **Story 2:** That's a balloon. It's bouncing. That's me. You know what? That's my playroom.
> **Story 3:** That's a balloon, but there are more. I blow balloons up this big (*child gestures with her arms*). It's a princess balloon.

During sessions, some children commented about the teacher writing down what they said. We noticed this in particular with dual language learners.

> A child from India is looking at her photo album.
> **Teacher:** That's great. Let me write down all these great words. So you said, "This is my brother pretending at the computer, and I am pretending I am the man."
> **Child:** Those are very long words for that (*pointing to some words in the story*).
> **Teacher:** That is a very long word. You are right.
> **Child:** And these are long words too (*pointing to several more words in the story*).

Suggestions for Using the Language Experience Approach

1. Choose a focus that is related to the children's lived experience. In our project, the children's photos of their worlds provided a wealth of conversational opportunities.
2. Ask children to share their thoughts, using gentle questioning that invites children's ideas rather than seeking answers.
3. Listen actively and provide wait time for the children to formulate their ideas.
4. Record the children's language. Use the children's own words, matching what they say with what you write. This demonstrates important print concepts.
5. Vary the type of record you create. LEA stories can become individual or class books, bulletin board signs, or illustrated posters. We carefully archived the children's stories in individual photo albums.
6. Revisit the stories often!

This approach supported children's concept development and vocabulary growth.

Conversations About the Photos Enrich All Children's Language

The children's strengthened voices conveyed messages about the world from the children's points of view.

Early childhood teachers want to understand each child and family. They seek to understand each child's family relationships, cultures, routines, and traditions and intentionally search for ways to assess each child's development.

As dual language learners described their photographs, we saw the power of the photos to strengthen each child's voice (Keat, Strickland, & Marinak 2009). If *voice* is the capacity to convey a message from one person's mind to another's, then the child-taken photographs provided the dual language learners with "microphones" that enhanced their ability to have their messages understood. Teachers heard the children's diverse voices in many ways.

First, the photographs helped the child focus the teacher's attention on a subject the child had selected. For example, one child, a dual language learner, patiently answered the teacher's questions about a photo for a few minutes and then stated, "I want to talk about that one now." The child directed the teacher's attention to a specific item and provided evidence of his social development as he noted the complexities of sharing: "This is mine that is actually Patrick's too. . . . Patrick always likes to play with this . . . but you have to shake it up first, and then you put it on the shelf." Another dual language learner said to the teacher, "Wait—that is my favorite," then explained several details that were important to him in a mini-story: "This is me. That is my mask. That is my costume for Halloween. I lost the mask; I had it, but now I can't find it."

Many years ago, Vivian Paley (1989) and the children in her classes taught us that "children have much to teach us if we will but stop and listen" (136). The children's strengthened voices conveyed messages about the world from the children's points of view.

The photos also evoked stories about the persons and pets the children loved, belongings they considered important, and activities they enjoyed. One dual language learner, who had spoken infrequently the previous year, carefully selected photographs and reported his feelings about each one: "I liked the instruments. I just like the instruments! That's Spunky. I love Spunky!" As the children described their affection for their pets, homes, and families, the teacher who listened sensitively could pick up details about each family's culture. "Suggestions for Listening to the Voices of Diverse Learners" (p. 31) provides a few suggestions we found helpful.

All too often, a familiar scene takes place in diverse classrooms. The teacher is working hard to bring a child who is a dual language learner into the class conversation. She attempts to engage the child, and the child responds with a smile and silence. The teacher's intent to care for and nurture the whole child is there, but something is in the way. Often the assumption is that the child's limited language skills are getting in the way of the teacher connecting with that child. However, is that the only obstacle?

Our investigation explored this very question. Armed with their photos and the teacher's attention, children taking part in this project received the time and space necessary to build the connections that helped them to begin sharing information about their lives. Though spending one-on-one time with children is always important, it was photo-narration and LEA processes that helped teachers connect with dual language learners. For example, a teacher explained her enhanced understanding of one child's home experiences: "I learned a lot about him. I learned that he loved helping his mom in the kitchen. I mean he had his own apron and his own set of miniature utensils. They must do it often, because they had all the stuff. If he spoke fluent English, I would have known all that much earlier."

During the project, we saw important connections that led us to take a closer look at the power of photo-narration. One of the most important connections voiced by the preschool teachers was that photo-narration gave them a view of the child's world. It provided new insights into how to connect with children from whom they felt disconnected. This "virtual tour" of a child's home, as one teacher called it, offered a glimpse into the child's world that was otherwise unknown and might have sometimes been misinterpreted. As one teacher noted with passion, "I can relate to a child on a more personal level when I am 'allowed' to see into parts of the child's world through the eyes of a camera—things that I probably would have never seen." Here are a few suggestions for connecting with diverse learners that emerged during debriefing conversations with our preschool colleagues: (1) be aware of your own assumptions; (2) listen actively—don't fill in the silent moments; and (3) be open to surprise.

Teachers' Reactions

In debriefing meetings with us during and after the project, our preschool colleagues noted that they learned more about all the children, particularly the dual language learners, than they initially had sought. They concluded that all children found the language experience approach meaningful and loved having their words written down. In the children's conversations, we found evidence that the preschoolers (a) shared their words, (b) demonstrated conceptual development and complex language, (c) recognized their words represented in print, (d) knew that the photos inspired their words, (e) corrected teachers when they did not transcribe their stories correctly, and (f) taught the teachers what was important to them (Nessel & Dixon 2008).

> **Suggestions for Listening to the Voices of Diverse Learners**
> 1. Lean toward the child to indicate interest.
> 2. Make eye contact with the child.
> 3. Wait quietly for a few moments after the child stops speaking to give the child thinking time.
> 4. Repeat the child's words slowly to let the child know that you heard.
> 5. Create a space in your mind that is empty of your own assumptions, so you can hear each child's way of understanding the world.

> "The one-to-one time was so valuable for me, to let the children know how special they were and how interested I was in hearing what they had to say."

Photo-narration using the language experience approach proved powerful and revealing for everyone involved in this collaboration. Perhaps two of our preschool colleagues captured conclusions better than we as researchers ever could:

> Once the cameras were sent home, I couldn't wait for them to come back so that the photos could be developed. I found that the children were just as excited as I was. It was such a great learning experience. I was able to meet with the children and listen to what they said as they went through their pictures. The camera was used as a tool to get a glimpse of their world outside of preschool. I really felt like I had a mini home visit with each of my students. The one-to-one time was so valuable for me, to let the children know how special they were and how interested I was in hearing what they had to say. Children who were quiet or those with limited English had a safe and meaningful reason to use their words. It was a great way to open up the lines of communication and conversation.
>
> —Colleen

> The cameras were a success. Needless to say, all the children loved setting out with their own cameras. The dual language learners did indeed find more language when they were talking about their pictures. The children would gather around each other to inspect, compare, and talk to each other about the photos.
>
> —Paula

Conclusion

At the conclusion of the study, the parents who were immigrants, contrary to the fears of the researchers and teachers, voiced how the children's being invited to take photos of the home communicated that the school valued them as a family. When asked about the process, they talked about their joy with the school and with teachers being so interested in their lives, even though they came from different cultural backgrounds.

By using photographs selected by the children and carefully recording their stories, the teachers began to hear the voices of the diverse learners (Clark 2007). As Alison Clark and Peter Moss (2011) so eloquently suggest, listening revealed the true mosaic of the children's lives. Any early childhood teacher can use the language experience approach and photo-narration to support the language and literacy development of all young learners. In our project, however, it proved especially powerful as a group of dedicated preschool teachers sought to connect with the dual language learners in their classrooms.

References

Allen, R. 1968. "How a Language Experience Program Works." In *A Decade of Innovations: Approaches to Beginning Reading*, ed. E.C. Vilscek, 1–8. Newark, DE: International Reading Association.

Clark, A. 2007. "A Hundred Ways of Listening: Gathering Children's Perspectives of Their Early Childhood Environment." *Young Children* 62 (3): 76–81.

Clark, A., & P. Moss. 2011. *Listening to Young Children: The Mosaic Approach.* 2nd ed. London: National Children's Bureau.

Clark-Ibáñez, M. 2004. "Framing the Social World With Photo-Elicitation Interviews." *American Behavioral Scientist* 47 (12): 1507–27.

Huey, E.B. [1908] 1968. *The Psychology and Pedagogy of Reading.* Cambridge, MA: MIT Press.

Keat, J., M. Strickland, & B. Marinak. 2009. "Child Voice: How Immigrant Children Enlightened Their Teachers With a Camera." *Early Childhood Education Journal* 37 (1): 13–21.

Labbo, L.D. 2005. "From Morning Message to Digital Morning Message: Moving From the Tried and True to the New." *The Reading Teacher* 58 (8): 782–5.

Lenters, K. 2004. "No Half Measures: Reading Instruction for Young Second-Language Learners." *The Reading Teacher* 58 (4): 328–36.

Marinak, B., M. Strickland, & J. Keat. 2009. "Using Cameras to Stimulate the Conversation of Native-Born and Immigrant Preschoolers." *Ubiquitous Learning: An International Journal* 1 (3): 7–11.

Nessel, D., & C. Dixon. 2008. *Using the Language Experience Approach With English Language Learners: Strategies for Engaging Students and Developing Literacy.* Thousand Oaks, CA: Sage.

Paley, V. 1989. *White Teacher.* Cambridge, MA: Harvard University Press.

Stauffer, R. 1970. *The Language-Experience Approach to the Teaching of Reading.* New York: Harper & Row.

Strickland, M., J. Keat, & B. Marinak. 2010. "Connecting Worlds: Using Photo Narrations to Connect Immigrant Children, Preschool Teachers, and Immigrant Families." *The School Community Journal* 20 (1): 81–102.

Cristina Gillanders and Dina C. Castro

Storybook Reading for Young Dual Language Learners

In a professional learning community meeting, teachers discuss their experiences reading aloud to dual language learners.

Susan: When I am reading a story, the Latino children in my class just sit there. They look at me, but you can tell that they are not engaged in the story.

Lisa: That happens in my class too. The little girls play with their hair, and the boys play with their shoes.

Beverly: And when you ask questions about the story, children who speak English take over and you can't get an answer from the Latino children.

Facilitator: What do you think is happening here?

Lisa: I think they just don't understand what the story is about.

Facilitator: How can we help them understand the story so they can participate?

Researchers widely recommend storybook reading for promoting the early language and literacy of young children. By listening to stories, children learn about written syntax and vocabulary, and they develop phonological awareness and concepts of print, all of which are closely linked to learning to read and write (National Early Literacy Panel 2008). Teachers usually know a read-aloud experience has been effective because they see the children maintain

naeyc® 2, 3

their interest in the story, relate different aspects of the story to their own experiences, describe the illustrations, and ask questions about the characters and plot.

However, listening to a story read aloud can be a very different experience for children who speak a language other than English. What happens when the children are read to in a language they are just beginning to learn? What happens when an English-speaking teacher reads a story to a group of children who are learning English as a second language?

As illustrated in the opening vignette, teachers often describe young dual language learners (DLLs) in their class as distracted and unengaged during read-aloud sessions in English. We describe teaching strategies that English-speaking teachers can use when reading aloud to young dual language learners. These strategies are part of the Nuestros Niños School Readiness Program, a professional development intervention designed to improve the quality of teaching practices in prekindergarten classrooms to support Spanish-speaking dual language learners (Castro et al. 2010).

The intervention was developed and evaluated in two studies with the participation of teachers from prekindergarten and Head Start programs in North Carolina, California, and Florida (Buysse, Castro, & Peisner-Feinberg 2010). The Nuestros Niños program responds to the immediate need to improve the practices that monolingual English-speaking early childhood teachers use when teaching young Latino dual language learners. Over the course of two full school years, the program included professional development institutes, classroom consultations, and professional learning communities meetings.

Nuestros Niños Professional Learning Communities

A professional learning community (PLC) allows teachers to work together to reflect and improve classroom practice with a focus on children's learning (DuFour 2004). In Nuestros Niños, we have used the lesson study model (Lewis 2002) to guide the systematic process of working collaboratively. To implement the lesson study process, teachers collectively plan, observe, analyze, and refine actual classroom lessons.

In the Nuestros Niños program, during the initial PLC meetings, the teachers defined their goals for the dual language learners in their classes and determined the theme (for example, insects, plants, or food) they would address with the storybook reading. Then they chose a picture book that had a Spanish version. They planned the storybook reading using the recommended strategies described later in this article. During this process, the authors of this article and Nuestros Niños facilitators worked with teachers to incorporate strategies that have been shown to be effective when teaching dual language learners.

The PLC group work produced a sample lesson plan. When the group had completed the lesson plan, one volunteer implemented it in her classroom while the other teachers observed the lesson or watched it on video. The PLC then revised the lesson plan to incorporate feedback from the observers. After the final revision, the other members of the group used the lesson plan in their classrooms. This process helped the teachers reflect on their own teaching practices and resulted in a carefully planned approach to using storybook reading to support dual language learners.

Cristina Gillanders, PhD, is a researcher at the FPG Child Development Institute at the University of North Carolina–Chapel Hill. She is a coprincipal investigator in the Nuestros Niños study, and has worked with dual language learners as a bilingual preschool teacher, teacher educator, and researcher.

Dina C. Castro, PhD, is a research professor at Mary Lou Teachers College, Arizona State University. She is the principal investigator for the Nuestros Niños study. Her research focuses on improving the quality of early education for children from diverse cultural and linguistic backgrounds.

Storybooks and DLL Vocabulary Development

One reason storybook reading is important for dual language learners is that it promotes vocabulary development. For most English-speaking children, vocabulary development in English occurs incidentally, that is, as a result of being exposed to new words when talking to family members, teachers, or friends, or when watching TV. For dual language learners, vocabulary development in English requires both incidental learning and direct teaching of words. Teachers can use storybook reading to combine direct teaching of new words with the use of the same words while reading aloud an engaging story.

Children who listen to stories in their own language can learn new words through active participation, such as answering questions related to the story. Dual language learners who have limited second language proficiency are not able to actively participate when books are read to them in English. So reading aloud to young dual language learners needs to be done in a way that allows the children to join in even if they are in the early stages of learning English.

When reading stories aloud, teachers can use strategies that maximize opportunities for children to understand the text, which will help them develop their vocabulary and listening comprehension. Storybook reading also promotes the development of other aspects of the language, such as the pronunciation of sounds of words (phonology), the correct construction of sentences (syntax), and the appropriate use of common phrases or expressions in English.

Recommended Strategies for Storybook Reading to Young DLLs

English-speaking teachers can adjust their approach to storybook reading when reading aloud to young dual language learners. By implementing the following strategies, early childhood educators can effectively reach these children. The sample lesson plan (see "Example of a Storybook-Reading Lesson Plan," pp. 38–39) uses the storybook *La Cucaracha Martina,* a Latin American folktale, and illustrates the strategies outlined in this article.

Choose a limited set of core words (three to five) and a repetitive phrase that are essential to understanding the story. Provide explicit instruction for learning the core words prior to and during the storybook-reading session. Ask questions

("Where is _____?" "What is he/she doing?"), point to illustrations, show objects, and use gestures. Include opportunities for children to repeat the words aloud, and define the words in terms the children can understand (Collins 2005, 2010).

Before reading the story aloud, introduce the core words using a picture walk. During a picture walk, the teacher takes the children through the book, pointing to the illustrations without reading the text. Use the repetitive phrase throughout the day during different classroom activities.

Use manipulatives, illustrations, gestures, and facial expressions to help children understand vocabulary (Echevarria, Short, & Peterson 2012). Invite children to be actively engaged in the storybook reading by asking them to show objects or pictures to the group at the appropriate time in the story.

Use the children's first language to facilitate story comprehension and English vocabulary acquisition. If you are bilingual or have some knowledge of the children's first language, read the story in the first language, and then on a subsequent occasion, read it in English (Lugo-Neris, Jackson, & Goldstein 2010).

If you are not fluent in the first language, ask a family member or other volunteer to read the story to the children in their first language. At the same time, ask your program to purchase several copies of this version of the book so you can send them home with children who are dual language learners, so families can read the story with them at home.

In addition, provide definitions of the core vocabulary words in English and the children's first language (in this case Spanish) on separate occasions (Lugo-Neris, Jackson, & Goldstein 2010). This facilitates children's learning of new words in English and Spanish. Teachers who are not fluent in the first language can find Spanish definitions of words in a dictionary or ask for help from Spanish-speaking parents or members of the community. Spanish definitions should also be included for families borrowing the book.

Read the story several times during the week. Listening to the story several times allows children to consolidate their learning and deepen their understanding of the words.

Incorporate culturally relevant thematic units and books. Children can use new vocabulary in the context of culturally familiar experiences as they play and learn in the classroom.

Be aware that dual language learners participate in storybook reading in different ways, depending on their phase of second language acquisition. If the children communicate only in their first language, expect that they might answer English-language questions in their first language. Teachers should learn some key words related to the story in the children's first language so that they can acknowledge children's efforts to communicate.

If the children who are dual language learners are not yet using oral language, it may mean that they are still in the phase of second language acquisition called the nonverbal period. During this period, dual language learners often participate by using gestures, pointing to illustrations, or showing objects.

Finally, if the children are beginning to use phrases in English, teachers can provide opportunities for them to complete a sentence or phrase and answer questions with a repetitive phrase.

Example of a Storybook-Reading Lesson Plan

Brooke Hackman, Janis Hart, Sheila Hamilton, Rhonda Privette, Patrice Ramsey, Tammy Smith, and Cristina Gillanders

La Cucaracha Martina, **by Daniel Moretón**

Story synopsis: While searching for the source of one beautiful sound, a pretty cockroach rejects marriage proposals from a collection of city animals who try to charm her with their noises.

Teacher Preparation

Gather materials

Props: Noisemaker, cockroach, lipstick, dog, pig, rooster, bird, snake, frog, duck, cat, mouse, bull, fish, ring, bee, cricket, and banjo

Picture cards for retelling: Cockroach, lipstick, dog, pig, rooster, bird, snake, frog, duck, cat, mouse, bull, fish, ring, bee, cricket, and banjo

Listening center: English and Spanish recordings of the story

Dramatic play area: Veils, neckties, and pictures of weddings

Science center: Books with realistic pictures of the animals in the story and a variety of plastic insects to sort

Sand and water table: Plastic insects and animals

Music center: A CD with loud noises and one with beautiful music, such as a piano solo

Reading center: Copies of *La Cucaracha Martina* in English and Spanish and animal puppets

Art center: A variety of art materials, including crayons, colored paper for collages, and markers

Identify core vocabulary

(Bold indicates words selected as the focus for the lesson.)

Cockroach / *cucaracha,* **noise** / *ruido,* **beautiful** / *hermoso,* dog / *perro,* pig / *puerco* / *cochino* / *marrano* / *chancho,* rooster / *gallo,* bird / *pájaro,* mouse / *ratón,* fish / *pescado* / *pez,* bull / *toro,* bee / *abeja,* **cricket** / *grillo,* flea / *pulga,* cat / *gato,* duck / *pato,* snake / *culebra* / *víbora,* frog / *sapo,* spider / *araña*

Choose a repetitive phrase

Will you marry me? / ¿Te quieres casar conmigo?

Plan ways to teach core vocabulary and the repetitive phrase before reading aloud

Cockroach / cucaracha: Show realistic pictures or a real cockroach for *cucaracha.* Sing the song, "La cucaracha." Define the word. For example, a cockroach is an insect that is brown and flat.

Noise / ruido: Play a recording of different noises, especially insect sounds. Use puppets or toys that make sounds. Define the word. For example, a noise is a sound that is unpleasant.

Beautiful / hermoso: Describe the colors used in a child's painting and listen to music, such as a violin solo, versus random noises. Define the word. For example, something beautiful is very pretty.

Cricket / grillo: Show realistic pictures of a cricket or observe crickets outside in the yard and describe them while repeating the word several times. Show toy or puppet crickets. Define the word. For example, a cricket is an insect that hops and chirps.

Repetitive phrase: Will you marry me? / ¿Te quieres casar conmigo? Show a wedding picture or album, reenact a wedding, do a wedding puppet show, watch a DVD of a wedding, or invite a family member to come and talk with the children about his/her wedding.

Encourage children to retell and to dramatize the story once they have heard it several times. This helps children to practice using the vocabulary words and helps them gain a better understanding of the story.

Expand the ideas in the book to other classroom centers. Using the core vocabulary words in other classroom learning centers provides opportunities for the children to use these words in various contexts in addition to the read-aloud.

Day 1: Picture walk

Introduce the book, saying, "We are going to read a new book this week. The title is *La Cucaracha Martina*. Before we talk about it, let's look at some important words."

Present the core words in print in English or Spanish and provide a brief explanation of their meaning by showing the following props: a toy that makes an annoying sound, a cockroach, a cricket, and a beautiful ring.

Ask leading questions during the picture walk, such as, "What kind of noises do you think she hears?," "What is the cucaracha doing in this picture?," "What animal did the cucaracha meet?"

Send home a copy of the Spanish version of the book for families to read with their children. You can also send home the English version of the book for families who speak English.

Day 2: Reading in Spanish

Invite a Spanish-speaking adult to read the book in Spanish to the whole group. Ask the reader to show the props while reading the story. Next, have the reader ask the children to name the animals that appear in the story and ask questions such as, "How do you think the cucaracha is feeling in this picture?," "What is the cucaracha doing in this picture?" Allow for answers in English and Spanish. If there are children in the class who do not speak Spanish, read the book in Spanish using the same strategies described in Day 3. This will allow the non-Spanish-speaking children to participate and understand the text.

Day 3: Reading in English

Introduce the book in English: "Today we are going to read the story *La Cucaracha Martina* again. This time I will need your help. I will give everybody a prop. Listen very carefully, and when we are reading the part that mentions the prop you have, put it in the middle of the circle."

Pass out the props, and then read the story. While you are reading, invite the children to put the props in the middle of the circle at the appropriate times. During the reading, encourage the children to recite the phrase "Will you marry me?," which is repeated throughout the story. At the end of the reading, ask, "What animals asked the cucaracha to marry them?," "Why doesn't she want to marry all these animals?," "Which animal did she want to marry?," "Why is the flea holding a ring?"

Day 4: Retelling

Encourage the children to use cards and a flannel board to retell the story, saying, "What is the name of the book we have been reading this week? Today we'll see what we remember and tell the story using picture cards on the flannel board." Pass out the cards with pictures of all the props used the previous day. Support the children as they retell the story and put the cards on the flannel board at the appropriate times.

Day 5: Dramatization

Encourage children to act out the story over several days. Invite families and guests to attend a presentation of the play.

Conclusion

Storybook reading can promote language and literacy development in young children, but teachers may need to adjust their practice when working with dual language learners. Teachers can use various strategies to support the children's comprehension of the text, which will in turn increase their participation in the lesson. This can help young dual language learners develop their vocabulary.

One important strategy is to introduce the text in the children's first, or dominant, language. Monolingual English-speaking teachers may find the use of the first language challenging. They can seek help from other program staff, the families of the children who are dual language learners, or other community members (for example, high school students taking advanced Spanish classes).

Effective use of these strategies requires careful planning, especially when teachers are learning to address the needs of young dual language learners. Working with fellow teachers in professional learning communities can provide support for the planning process as well as an opportunity for teachers to reflect on teaching, its challenges, and opportunities for professional growth.

References

Buysse, V., D.C. Castro, & E. Peisner-Feinberg. 2010. "Effects of a Professional Development Program on Classroom Practices and Outcomes for Latino Dual Language Learners." *Early Childhood Research Quarterly* 25 (2): 194–206.

Castro, D.C., C. Gillanders, X. Franco, & M. Zepeda. 2010. *Nuestros Niños: School Readiness Program*. Participant manual. Chapel Hill: The University of North Carolina, FPG Child Development Institute.

Collins, M.F. 2005. "ESL Preschoolers' English Vocabulary Acquisition From Storybook Reading." *Reading Research Quarterly* 40 (4): 406–8.

Collins, M.F. 2010. "ELL Preschoolers' English Vocabulary Acquisition From Storybook Reading." *Early Childhood Research Quarterly* 25 (1): 84–97.

DuFour, R. 2004. "What Is a Professional Learning Community?" *Educational Leadership* 61 (8): 6–11.

Echevarria, J., D.J. Short, & C. Peterson. 2012. *Using the SIOP Model With Pre-K and Kindergarten English Learners*. New York: Pearson.

Lewis, C. 2002. *Lesson Study: A Handbook of Teacher-Led Instructional Change*. Philadelphia: Research for Better Schools.

Lugo-Neris, M., C.W. Jackson, & H. Goldstein. 2010. "Facilitating Vocabulary Acquisition of Young English Language Learners." *Language, Speech & Hearing Services in Schools* 41 (3): 314–27.

National Early Literacy Panel. 2008. *Developing Early Literacy: Report of the National Early Literacy Panel*. Washington, DC: National Institute for Literacy. http://lincs.ed.gov/publications/pdf/NELPReport09.pdf.

Ben Mardell,
Marina Boni, and
Jason Sachs

Vivian Paley's Storytelling/Story Acting Comes to the Boston Public Schools

naeyc® 2, 3

Vivian Paley shared stories from her rich career as a preschool and kindergarten teacher in her keynote address at NAEYC's 2011 Annual Conference. She then asked us to imagine a world without stories. Such a world would be an impoverished place indeed.

Stories are vital to children's understanding of the world. Paley's determination to make stories an important part of children's lives took shape in her kindergarten classroom more than 40 years ago, when she initiated a program that has become known as storytelling/story acting (ST/SA). In ST/SA a child dictates a story and the class then dramatizes it (Paley 1981, 1991, 1997). Teachers worldwide embrace storytelling and story acting. For example,

Houston (see School Literacy and Culture 2013) and London (see MakeBelieve Arts 2013) are notable for the large scale of their efforts. And the Boston school district makes ST/SA part of its early childhood curriculum.

Boston Public Schools (BPS) is an ethnically and culturally diverse system, with some 45 percent of the students being dual language learners (DLLs). During the 2012–2013 school year, the Boston school district piloted storytelling/story acting in 50 kindergarten classrooms. Now part of Focus on K2, the Boston kindergarten curriculum, the ST/SA component is called Boston Listens. The curriculum is being phased in during the 2013–2015 school years and

Ben Mardell, PhD, is a professor of early childhood education at Lesley University in Cambridge, Massachusetts. He works with Boston Public School teachers to promote children's creativity and literacy and language development in democratic classroom communities.

Marina Boni, MS, is a program developer for early childhood education in the Boston Public Schools. She mentors teachers in K1 and K2 and facilitates professional development.

Jason Sachs, EdD, is the director of early childhood education for the Boston Public Schools.

introduced in all 250 BPS kindergartens, which include children with special needs. Soon more than 4,000 young learners will be telling their stories and acting them out in Boston schools.

In addition to the basics of storytelling/story acting, BPS's version includes three special components: adult stories, communication, and family engagement. After briefly describing storytelling/story acting and these three components, the authors explain the ways ST/SA promotes kindergartners' learning, how it benefits children learning English, and how it benefits children with special needs. They discuss some of the challenges confronting Boston public school kindergarten teachers and how they met them. To provide more detail on the content, they refer readers to relevant websites for the Boston ST/SA program. (See "The BPS Early Childhood Website.")

Storytelling/Story Acting

Dictation and dramatization are the core of ST/SA. Using their experiences and imaginations, children individually tell their own stories to an adult, who writes them down. At group time the teacher reads the stories aloud as children act them out. ST/SA requires few materials: paper, a pencil or pen, and a clipboard. Some teachers provide individual binders or notebooks in which children collect their stories. For dramatization, children need an area where they can sit comfortably in a circle, with space in the middle for the story acting.

Storytelling (Dictation)

Supporting children's storytelling involves teachers' careful listening and gentle scaffolding, such as asking clarifying questions. It is an opportunity to engage children one-on-one in a joyful activity. Some children may begin the year telling lengthy stories, while others' stories may be very short. However, even a one-word story should be celebrated and acted out. In the BPS curriculum, stories are limited to one page, allowing time for more stories and dramatizations.

During story dictation "teacherly moments" arise. Children watch intently as teachers write down their words. They may ask about punctuation or particular words, leading to conversations about question marks and initial consonants. However, it is critical that ST/SA not be turned into a phonics lesson. The teacher's primary role in dictation is listener.

See video examples of scaffolding and tools to support children's storytelling.
http://bpsearlychildhood.weebly.com/dictation.html

Story Acting (Dramatization)

By bringing children's stories to the group, story acting honors children's ideas. It gives children a compelling reason to tell stories and an opportunity to create meaning around an authentic narrative they are interested in. Story acting allows children to learn from one another as they creatively figure out how to depict a cat, a princess, or even a tissue box (true story!). Teachers learn more about the children as they work together to bring children's stories to life.

During dictation the story's author has chosen her own role, and this is announced to the group. The teacher then begins reading the story. When the first character appears, she invites a child to enter the ST/SA designated area to take that part. If the child declines the invitation, the teacher proceeds to the next child in the circle. Each time a new character appears, the teacher, continuing around the circle, asks the next child to act: "Can I see you be the neighbor?" Using this language encourages children to decide independently how to portray the characters. Teachers should be expansive in their definition of characters—to allow the maximum number of children to participate in a dramatization, characters can include elements like houses, trees, and pets.

When story acting is about to take place, teachers find that rituals, such as ringing a bell, help build excitement and focus the audience's attention. Inviting the children to co-construct such rituals promotes a democratic classroom culture by involving children in decisions about their learning. For example, children might suggest applauding a dramatization, if the author is comfortable accepting applause.

> Watch videos on the first web page that illustrate aspects of the dramatization process. Visit the second for video clips of Vivian Paley and Trish Lee discussing ST/SA.
> **http://bpsearlychildhood.weebly.com/dramatization.html**
> **http://bpsearlychildhood.weebly.com/the-wisdom-of-vivian-paley-and-trish-lee.html**

Treated as literature, children's stories can be the basis for valuable conversations. Ask children to share their impressions of stories and to make connections with other areas of the curriculum and with their own experiences. Include terms such as *characters, setting, plot,* and *suspense* in the conversations. You might also ask the children in the audience what they enjoyed about a performance and whether they have any suggestions for the cast.

Adults' Stories

The stories adults tell provide models for children—ideas about characters, plot, and narrative structure. These oral stories can be told at any time during the day by teachers, paraprofessionals, administrators, or family members. Children rarely copy these models directly, but rather mine them for ideas. Adults' stories promote a classroom culture of storytelling, inspiring children to share their stories with classmates.

Adults might base their stories on personal experiences (children love to hear stories about their teachers' lives), folktales or fairy tales (The Three Billy Goats Gruff, Abiyoyo), or imaginary tales they create (the children solving a mystery).

> Find examples of stories to tell children and suggestions for increasing children's engagement.
> **http://bpsearlychildhood.weebly.com/modeling-storytelling.html**

Communication

After children have dictated and dramatized their stories, teachers may offer additional opportunities for them to enjoy the stories and communicate their ideas. For example, children might illustrate their stories. Teachers can display the drawings on a bulletin board, put them in an ever growing binder of classroom stories (that are read by children, teachers, and classroom guests), or place them in children's individual portfolios. Stories can also inspire collage making or painting and suggest themes for block constructions.

Teachers might consider making video or audio recordings of dramatizations. Children enjoy watching recorded performances and, if transcripts are available, can follow the print as they play the recordings.

> See examples of children's stories displayed in different ways.
> http://bpsearlychildhood.weebly.com/communication.html

Family Engagement

As children's first teachers, families can support their children's learning through stories. Teachers can encourage families to tell stories (at home, for example, or on a car ride to the grocery store) about their day, their childhood, or their favorite tales when they were young, and to listen to their children's stories. Teachers can also invite family members to share their stories at school. It is important for teachers to explain to families how stories support children's success in school (see the section that follows, "How ST/SA Promotes Learning").

> Find a family-friendly fact sheet, a sample newsletter, and a video for families explaining how ST/SA supports children's learning. Also read details of a successful story event held at the Blackstone School.
> http://bpsearlychildhood.weebly.com/family-engagement.html

How ST/SA Promotes Learning

Because storytelling/story acting is based on stories and on play—two elements of the world that a young child finds most interesting—it is very engaging. With children's engagement come important benefits in cognitive learning and social and emotional development.

Language and Literacy Skills

Vocabulary. A robust vocabulary is essential for children's reading comprehension and their success in school (NICHD 2000). ST/SA provides a rich context for vocabulary development as children listen to and use words in authentic ways. During this activity, children frequently ask about the meaning of words, and teachers can suggest more specific vocabulary. Dramatization brings words to life. It is not surprising that children who participate in story dictation (McCabe et al. 2009) and ST/SA (Cooper et al. 2007) score higher on the Peabody Picture Vocabulary Test (Dunn & Dunn 2007) than peers from comparable socioeconomic and linguistic backgrounds who do not participate.

Narrative structure. Narrative abilities are also essential for success in reading and writing, and ST/SA provides a bridge between the contextualized speech of young children and the decontextualized language of books and writing (Snow 1983). That is, most young children's speech is about the here and now: children tell us, "I don't like *that,*" "I want *it,*" and "*He* hit me." Contextual cues—children pointing, adults surveying the environment, and people participating in shared experiences—support such conversations.

ST/SA is like the written word in that the stories are generally set outside the immediate context (the classroom). However, ST/SA offers contextual cues—tone of voice, gesture, movement—all of which help convey the meaning of the words. In this way ST/SA acts as a bridge between the contextual language of early childhood and the more abstract language of literacy.

Narrative development is a strong predictor of success in reading and writing; 4-year-olds with more advanced narrative skills are stronger fourth and eighth grade readers than those without (Snow, Burns, & Griffin 1998). McNamee (1987) found that participating in ST/SA promotes essential narrative abilities, a finding confirmed by Nicolopoulou and Cole (2010).

Print awareness and phonemic awareness. ST/SA supports literacy skills such as print awareness and phonemic awareness (Cooper 2005; Nicolopoulou 2008; Cremin et al. 2013). During story dictation, children notice the left-to-right and top-to-bottom directions of print when they watch the teacher transcribe their words. They attend to features of letters, their sounds, and the spelling of favorite words. Seeing print used for a meaningful purpose such as storytelling, children are motivated to begin writing themselves (Nicolopoulou, McDowell, & Brockmeyer 2006; Cremin et al. 2013).

Social and Emotional Development

Self-esteem. Some children come to school confident and ready to interact with peers. Others, because of shyness or special needs, may be more reserved. ST/SA takes all children's ideas seriously. Their ideas become known and are celebrated. Through mastery of telling and acting out stories children's confidence increases, and teachers note that children are more willing to participate in discussions after the implementation of a storytelling/story acting program (Cremin et al. 2013).

Community building. ST/SA fosters a sense of belonging and of social connection (Cremin et al. 2013). In *The Boy Who Would Be a Helicopter*, Vivian Paley (1991) tells of Jason, a child who initially did not fit in with the other children in the classroom. Through participation in ST/SA, Paley and Jason's classmates forged bonds with Jason that drew him into the classroom community.

Chris Bucco, a BPS prekindergarten teacher, saw similar results with several children in the class identified as being on the autism spectrum. Through ST/SA Chris gave these children strategies to enter play groups, thus integrating them into the blocks and dramatic play areas and enriching the entire classroom community (Mardell et al. 2010).

Self-regulation. Learning self-regulation—to wait, take turns, and defer—is a major task of early childhood (Berk, Mann, & Ogan 2006) and is important to later school success (McClelland et al. 2013). ST/SA promotes self-regulation by giving young children a compelling reason to take turns and follow rules (Nicolopoulou, McDowell, & Brockmeyer 2006).

> Listen to kindergartners themselves explain how ST/SA teaches self-regulation.
>
> **http://bpsearlychildhood.weebly.com/storytelling.html**

Creativity

Eleanor Duckworth (2006) observes that "the more we help children have their wonderful ideas and to feel good about themselves for having them, the more likely it is that they will someday happen upon wonderful ideas that no one else has happened upon before" (14). From figuring out how to act like a dinosaur or a flower to telling a meaningful one-word story, ST/SA affords numerous opportunities for children to have wonderful ideas and to feel good about themselves. Cremin and her colleagues (2013) report that classrooms that introduce ST/SA see an increase in children having innovative and original ideas.

The experience of Jackson, a kindergartner who was a dual language learner, exemplifies the value of ST/SA. Seeing Jackson begin the school year shy and reserved, his teacher eventually coaxed him to dictate a story. This was Jackson's first story:

> It was somebody's birthday. I don't know who. I don't know whose birthday it is. It's not me. But it's somebody's birthday. That's it.

As Jackson watched his stories and his classmates' stories being dramatized over time, his interest in the activity increased. He became an enthusiastic actor and eagerly awaited his turn to tell a story. Through listening and speaking, his vocabulary and narrative abilities blossomed. This is clear in his final story of the school year:

> Once upon a time we were in the veterinary clinic. There was Douglas, Dimas, and Ashley. We weighed the cats. We measured them with the tape. We gave them a bath and food. We were taking care of them. Then a cat died. The doctor came and took him away. He was gone. Then the doctor brought him back to life. The end.

Supporting Dual Language Learners and Children With Special Needs

The nonverbal elements of storytelling/story acting offer children learning English and children with special needs opportunities to participate in classroom life. In fact, ST/SA incorporates curricular elements that experts recommend to support dual language learning—allowing frequent chances to talk, making connections to children's lives, and exploring interesting topics (Haneda & Wells 2012).

Yet the verbal aspects of ST/SA mean that the stories told by DLLs and by children with special needs may differ from the stories of native English speakers and children who do not have special needs. Early in the program, some children may be hesitant to tell stories. Storytelling should always be a choice. Experience shows that over time almost all children choose to tell stories.

While it is important not to view learning English as a special need, the verbal elements of ST/SA mean that children learning English and children with special needs benefit from similar supports. These supports include teachers doing the following:

- **Accepting short stories.** Honoring very short stories—even one-word stories—encourages children to become more confident and to grow as storytellers.

- **Modeling storytelling and story acting.** Children learning English often use teachers' stories as models for their own tales.

- **Offering prompts based on observation.** By observing children at play, teachers come to know them better. When children have difficulty beginning a story or expressing themselves, teachers can gently scaffold, making suggestions based on such knowledge.
- **Providing visual props.** Mayer-Johnson boardmaker images, puppets, and felt boards are vehicles children can use to help tell their stories, pointing to and manipulating them to illustrate their ideas.
- **Going to the story.** Children who are hesitant to tell a story may be creating complex narratives in the block area or during dramatic play. Instead of asking such children to come over to a table, teachers can go to the places reticent children are playing to get their dictation.

While most children tell stories independently, supports like these allow teachers to co-construct stories with children who need assistance.

> Find further suggestions from BPS teachers about supporting children with a range of abilities, needs, and proficiencies in English.
> **http://bpsearlychildhood.weebly.com/boston-listens-seminar.html**

Teacher Challenges and Strategies

The core components of storytelling/story acting are straightforward—take a story and act it out. Its simplicity belies the fact that working with young children is complex. During the pilot year, teachers encountered challenges and devised strategies to overcome them. The challenges included addressing children's stories containing violence, supplying the appropriate level of scaffolding, and making time in the routine to conduct ST/SA.

Addressing Violence in Stories

The issue of violence in children's stories and play has long been controversial. Some children are exposed daily to violence. And in communities where guns and fighting are all too present, it is particularly disturbing to see children acting out shooting and killing. Yet many children are drawn to superhero play, and violence has long been a feature of young children's stories (see Goodenough & Prelinger 1963).

When children told stories that included violence, BPS teachers had to decide how to respond. Teacher conversations led to a consensus to allow stories with fighting and violence. Teachers understood that stories are a way children make sense of the world. They were swayed by Vivian Paley's argument that by helping children safely dramatize such stories, teachers help them learn that they control the story, not the other way around.

However, this was not the end of the conversation. Despite the decision to allow such stories, many teachers still felt uncomfortable. Some admitted that they rushed the children through dramatizations of stories with fighting and violence, and wondered whether the children realized that teachers valued other themes more highly.

For example, Sarae Pacetta, a visiting artist, brought the issue of children's stories containing violence to the attention of a group of teachers in an early childhood workshop, along with a video of the dramatization of a superhero story she had facilitated. The

> View the first video to hear Vivian Paley discuss how to address violent themes in children's stories.
> **http://bpsearlychildhood.weebly.com/the-wisdom-of-vivian-paley-and-trish-lee.html**

teachers' collective analysis of the video helped Sarae and her colleagues gain a deeper appreciation for the learning that occurs during such dramatizations. Not only did the children involved not hurt each other as they pretended to fight, but they engaged in an elaborate choreography that involved much coordination and thought. The teachers concluded that they should be more open to story themes often favored by boys. (To view the video and hear the analysis, see point number six at the previously noted web page.)

Scaffolding

Beyond writing down children's words, the teacher's role in dictation is subject to some debate. Some proponents of ST/SA, like Trish Lee (who introduced ST/SA in England—to learn more, visit the previously noted web page), maintain that teachers should act merely as scribes and not offer any input during dictation. They worry that questioning undermines children's ownership of (and ultimately their interest in) storytelling, and assert that children's narratives develop without adult prompting.

BPS educators embrace the notion that in dictation, a teacher's role is to provide gentle scaffolding, asking children questions such as, "Does anything else happen?," "What did [a character] do then?," and "How did you feel when that happened?" This means asking only a few questions during a dictation session; dictation should never resemble a cross-examination. It's important to note that teachers' questions are motivated by curiosity and the desire to better understand the storyteller's thinking. The input of peers who may be present during dictation can also serve as gentle scaffolding.

A teacher consideration in understanding the way children tell stories is the influence of their cultural backgrounds (McCabe 1997). Cultures have different ways of organizing stories, and teachers unfamiliar with a particular cultural style of storytelling may evaluate children's stories as underdeveloped or disorganized. For example, some African American children tell stories of interconnected events rather than stories with a beginning, middle, and end (McCabe 1997). BPS teachers learn about the different narrative styles of the cultures represented in the class and keep them in mind as they support individual children's storytelling.

Making Time for ST/SA

Even though storytelling/story acting does not require a great deal of time (about five minutes for each dictation and three minutes for a dramatization), finding time for four or five stories can be a challenge. BPS teachers include a dedicated time—approximately

20 minutes—for ST/SA in their daily schedules, offering children predictability and ensuring that the activity takes place. Administrative support is critical for ST/SA to be understood not as an extra to be squeezed in, but as an important part of the kindergarten curriculum.

The Importance of Making Stories Visible Beyond Classroom Walls

Key stakeholders (educators, families, policy makers, community leaders) need to understand the value of storytelling/story acting within the dynamic of an American, urban, public school system. This is important because, despite the research demonstrating the program's educational benefits, ST/SA has a public relations problem—children think it's fun. In today's educational climate, where rigor is a byword, those not familiar with early childhood development may wonder about the value of an activity based in story and play.

Researchers (Cremin et al. 2013) recommend cultivating stakeholders' understanding of the benefits of ST/SA by (1) clearly aligning ST/SA with existing standards (such as the Common Core State Standards [www.corestandards.org] or the NAEYC Early Childhood Program Standards and Criteria [NAEYC 2007]); (2) articulating the ways ST/SA promotes language and literacy development; and (3) creating materials specifically for policy makers explaining why ST/SA is important.

> Find teacher and administrator guides related to the BPS storytelling/story acting program.
> **http://bpsearlychildhood.weebly.com/guides.html**

Along with following these three recommendations, BPS educators have also made children's learning through ST/SA visible outside the classroom. On two evenings in the program's pilot year, the Boston Children's Museum hosted 100 children and their teachers from 13 different classrooms on the Kids' Stage (a child-friendly theater in the museum). The children dramatized selected stories for their extended families and community members. Like storytelling/story acting in the classroom, this was a magical experience. Making the learning of ST/SA visible has supported efforts to expand its use to Boston Public Schools first and second grade classrooms, providing young children with a deeper experience that will give meaning to their literacy learning throughout school and life.

> View a video clip of the Boston Children's Museum ST/SA event.
> **http://bpsearlychildhood.weebly.com/storytelling.html**

References

Berk, L.E., T.D. Mann, & A.T. Ogan. 2006. "Make-Believe Play: Wellspring for Development of Self-Regulation." Chap. 5 in *Play = Learning: How Play Motivates and Enhances Children's Cognitive and Social-Emotional Growth,* eds. D.G. Singer, R.M. Golinkoff, & K. Hirsh-Pasek. New York: Oxford University Press.

Cooper, P. 2005. "Literacy Learning and Pedagogical Purpose in Vivian Paley's 'Storytelling Curriculum.'" *Journal of Early Childhood Literacy* 5 (3): 229–51.

Cooper, P., K. Capo, B. Mathes, & L. Gray. 2007. "One Authentic Early Literacy Practice and Three Standardized Tests: Can a Storytelling Curriculum Measure Up?" *Journal of Early Childhood Teacher Education* 28 (3): 251–75.

Cremin, T., J. Swann, R. Flewitt, D. Faulkner, & N. Kucirkova. 2013. *Evaluation Report of MakeBelieve Arts Helicopter Technique of Storytelling and Story Acting.* London: MakeBelieve Arts. www.makebelievearts.co.uk/docs/Helicopter-Technique-Evaluation.pdf.

Duckworth, E.R. 2006. *"The Having of Wonderful Ideas" and Other Essays on Teaching and Learning.* New York: Teachers College Press.

Dunn, L.M., & D.M. Dunn. 2007. *Peabody Picture Vocabulary Test.* 4th ed. Boston, MA: Pearson.

Goodenough, E., & E.P. Prelinger. 1963. *Children Tell Stories: An Analysis of Fantasy.* New York: International Universities Press.

Haneda, M., & G. Wells. 2012. "Some Key Pedagogic Principles for Helping ELLs to Succeed in School." *Theory Into Practice* 51 (4): 297–304.

MakeBelieve Arts. 2013. *Helicopter.* www.makebelievearts.co.uk/Helicopter.

Mardell, B., L. Fiore, M. Boni, & M. Tonachel. 2010. "The Rights of Children: Policies to Best Serve 3, 4, and 5 Year Olds in Public Schools." *Scholarlypartnershipsedu* 5 (1): Article 5. http://opus.ipfw.edu/spe/vol5/iss1/5.

McCabe, A. 1997. "Cultural Background and Storytelling: A Review and Implications for Schooling." *The Elementary School Journal* 97 (5): 453–73.

McCabe, A., J. Boccia, M.B. Bennett, N. Lyman, & R. Hagan. 2009. "Improving Oral Language and Literacy Skills in Preschool Children From Disadvantaged Backgrounds: Remembering, Writing, Reading (RWR)." *Imagination, Cognition and Personality* 29 (4): 363–90.

McClelland, M.M., A.C. Acock, A. Piccinin, S.A. Rhea, & M.C. Stallings. 2013. "Relations Between Preschool Attention Span-Persistence and Age 25 Educational Outcomes." *Early Childhood Research Quarterly* 28 (2): 314–24.

McNamee, G.D. 1987. "The Social Origins of Narrative Skills." Chap. 14 in *Social and Functional Approaches to Language and Thought,* ed. M. Hickmann. Orlando, FL: Academic Press.

NAEYC. 2007. *NAEYC Early Childhood Program Standards and Accreditation Criteria: The Mark of Quality in Early Childhood Education.* Washington, DC: NAEYC.

NICHD (National Institute of Child Health and Development). 2000. *Teaching Children to Read: An Evidence-Based Assessment of the Scientific Research Literature on Reading and Its Implications for Reading Instruction.* A report of the National Reading Panel. (NIH Pub. No. 00-4754.) Washington, DC: Government Printing Office. www.dys-add.com/resources/SpecialEd/TeachingChildrenToRead.pdf.

Nicolopoulou, A. 2008. "The Elementary Forms of Narrative Coherence in Young Children's Storytelling." *Narrative Inquiry* 18 (2): 299–325. www.cas.lehigh.edu/CASWeb/resource.aspx?id=1202.

Nicolopoulou, A., J. McDowell, & C. Brockmeyer. 2006. "Narrative Play and Emergent Literacy: Storytelling and Story-Acting Meet Journal Writing." Chap. 7 in *Play = Learning: How Play Motivates and Enhances Children's Cognitive and Social-Emotional Growth,* eds. D.G. Singer, R.M. Golinkoff, & K. Hirsh-Pasek. New York: Oxford University Press.

Nicolopoulou, A., & M. Cole. 2010. "Design Experimentation as a Theoretical and Empirical Tool for Developmental Pedagogical Research." *Pedagogies: An International Journal* 5 (1): 61–71.

Paley, V.G. 1981. *Wally's Stories: Conversations in Kindergarten.* Cambridge, MA: Harvard University Press.

Paley, V.G. 1991. *The Boy Who Would Be a Helicopter: The Uses of Storytelling in the Classroom.* Cambridge, MA: Harvard University Press.

Paley, V.G. 1997. *The Girl With the Brown Crayon: How Children Use Stories to Shape Their Lives.* Cambridge, MA: Harvard University Press.

School Literacy and Culture, Rice University. 2011. "Classroom Storytelling Project." http://centerforeducation.rice.edu/slc/csp.html.

Snow, C.E. 1983. "Literacy and Language: Relationships During the Preschool Years." *Harvard Educational Review* 53 (2): 165–89.

Snow, C.E., M.S. Burns, & P. Griffin, eds. 1998. *Preventing Reading Difficulties in Young Children.* A report of the National Research Council. Washington, DC: National Academy Press. www.nap.edu/catalog.php?record_id=6023.

Ruth Shagoury

Language to Language: Nurturing Writing Development in Multilingual Classrooms

I sit in a small circle with several 5-year-olds as they pore through their writing journals to share pieces that are ready for publication on the writing wall. The children have created a thoughtful process for inviting two mostly silent friends into the conversation about writing. One of those children, Mariaevelyn, rarely ventures words even in her native Spanish. The other child, Lyuba, just now beginning to mouth a word or two of either Russian or English, smiles her way through the day.

Nonetheless, they actively participate in the group conference. As Katie, David, and Tonia share their writing, they pass their journals over to Mariaevelyn and Lyuba. Each of these girls, in turn, ponders the page, and then points to a section of the journal with a detail that she likes.

"Oh, you like the words?" Katie asks, as she follows Lyuba's pointed finger.
Lyuba nods.
Mariaevelyn likes the big yellow sun, and points to the upper right-hand corner.
"I like the sun part too," Katie confirms. "And I can make a rainbow."

naeyc ® 2, 3, 4

C
ommunity—one of the intangibles that make a classroom run smoothly— helps welcome all learners to the daily work. As children with diverse backgrounds, cultures, and languages come together in learning environments from preschool on, it is vital that each person initiate actions that invite others' voices into the mix.

Creating a literate classroom environment that nurtures the writing development of dual language learners (DLLs) requires more than presenting a series of skills to learn or academics to master. Classrooms should also be dedicated to building on children's knowledge, experience, and needs and to helping them acquire shared knowledge and understandings about what literacy is and how it can be a gift for communicating and learning.

Ruth Shagoury, PhD, is a literacy professor at Lewis & Clark College in Portland, Oregon, where she teaches, researches, and coordinates the language and literacy program. She works with students of all ages, from preschool through adult.

Children's work samples courtesy of the author.

Classroom Context

As a university literacy researcher, I have been investigating what is possible for dual language learners as they acquire literacy skills. For four years, I was embedded in Andie Cunningham's multilingual kindergarten class, a classroom in which at least six different languages were spoken (Cunningham & Shagoury 2005). As I looked more closely at the children's beginning reading skills, I came to appreciate the importance of written language to their overall literacy growth, thus shifting my focus to written language acquisition and development. To extend my research, I spent two years in Head Start classrooms with preschool multilingual children. These young learners taught me what is possible for preschool children to accomplish in terms of written language development.

The majority of research that focuses on children's writing is based on children whose home language is English. But more specific study of young dual language learners as they develop as writers is taking place. In her book *When English Language Learners Write,* Katharine Samway concludes that "the most current research shows that non-native English-speaking children are capable of much more than is generally expected of them" (2006, 22).

Children's Writing Samples

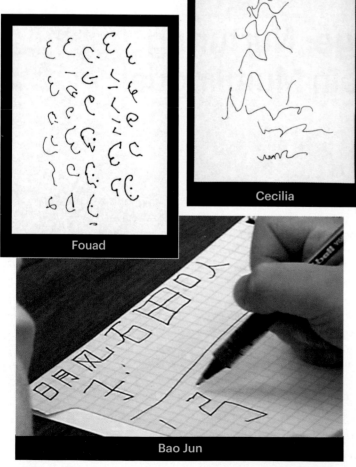

Fouad

Cecilia

Bao Jun

Young Dual Language Learners' Awareness of Print

Young children across languages and cultures reveal an awareness of the particular written features of their home languages (Sebba 2007). Four-year-old Fouad's Arabic writing, for example, has lots of dots and squiggles, which he reads back in Arabic. Five-year-old Bao Jun's Chinese writing shows logographic characteristics. Both children also make shapes that represent the English alphabet that they see around them. Even very early scribble writing, such as 3-year-old Cecilia's, is reflective of cursive English (see "Children's Writing Samples," p. 52).

Bilingual children immersed in dual languages at home since birth sort out the two languages, creating hypotheses about how to speak both. In the same way, young dual language learners actively figure out the way written language works in their first and second languages. Katharine Samway (2006) stresses the need for dual language learners to have access to what she calls "the creative construction principle" to allow their writing to emerge. In other words, children need the chance to explore how written language works in different situations, continually trying out their hypotheses. Paying attention to young children's first writing attempts means honoring ways they use the symbols they create to make meaning. It also means paying attention to the content as it provides a window into children's minds, which allows teachers to discover what is happening in their worlds and what is significant to them (Shagoury 2009).

Five-year-old Song enters kindergarten in the fall, speaking a few words, phrases, and expressions in English. Hmong is the language she and her family speak at home, although their English language skills are strong enough that they do not need translators at parent conferences.

Since there are no other Hmong speakers in Song's class, nor ethnic Hmong aides or translators at the school, English is what Song uses to communicate with her friends at school. She is by no means silent, although often quiet. She relies on gestures, pictures, and simple phrases and sentences in English to get her meaning across.

Song's literacy grows steadily over the school year. In the fall, she draws many pictures and makes a gradual transition to adding letters to go with them. She also copies letters from the English and Spanish words she sees in the classroom environment. By May, Song begins to use letters to represent sounds. In her drawing of the water in a river [see "Song's Writing"], she uses an r for the /r/ sound. And on the very same page, she uses a string of Chinese characters, which, she tells us, is the kind of writing her parents do.

Song's Writing

Song's growing literacy in two languages seemed to help shore up her confidence to share her at-home writing with us in school. By June she experimented with exclamation marks, voice bubbles, and spaces between words, and she wrote several books to share with friends. The classroom environment allowed Song the time and space to be an active and creative written language user.

Writing Right From the Start

Song is not an exception. Dual language learners can write before orally mastering the English language (Freeman & Freeman 2006; Samway 2006; Sebba 2007; Shagoury 2009). Just like other children, dual language learners write before they can read, and they use drawing to explore their ideas and thinking.

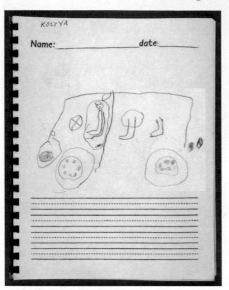

Kostya's Drawing

Russian-speaking Kostya comes to kindergarten speaking no English but is very willing to use gestures and facial expressions to communicate with adults and classmates. He usually looks very serious when he opens his writing journal and sits down to write—with intention.

One morning, his story is about the truck his father drives [see "Kostya's Drawing"]. Like all good writers, Kostya uses detail in his piece—from lug nuts in the tires to the steering wheel, to the exhaust floating out at the vehicle's rear. He even includes the passengers' arms dangling out of the windows.

When asked about his drawing, Kostya explains in Russian. But knowing I cannot understand, he supplements his verbal explanation with pointing, movement, and gesture. Our exchange of conversation helps his language development, as I continue to guess his meaning, supplying English words for *car* (he shakes his head no), and *bus* (no again, but with a smile this time). But then I am rewarded with an emphatic yes when I offer the word *truck*.

"Yes, truck!" he repeats, which draws his neighbors, Luis and Tony, into our conversation.

What is the role of talk in developing dual language learners' emerging literacy? Researchers Ernst and Richard (1995) found that talk is indeed an important influence on preschool and early elementary children's developing oral and written fluency in English. Writing and drawing are conversation starters that help children share interests and their own stories in response to each other (Samway 2006; Shagoury 2009).

The Role of Home Languages in Writing Development

Bilingual programs have an obvious advantage. Research shows that children who learn literacy in their first language do not need to relearn these skills in the second language. That is, dual language learners who learn to read in their home language do not need to be taught to read in English; they simply transfer the skills to their second language. The same holds true for writing (Garcia & Kleifgen 2010; Freeman & Freeman 2011).

In diverse schools in which children speak many languages, it is not feasible to create bilingual programs for every language. But whenever possible, it is beneficial to find speakers to talk and write with young children in their home language.

Kindergartner Alma writes a complex story in pictures. She starts to write out sounds to label the story. *Cat* and *twins* are the two English words that stand out in her story. In an attempt to support her, a classroom helper dictates letters to her. These are not words Alma can read back, so she turns from this story in frustration. But the classroom's bilingual aide encourages Alma to tell her story in Spanish, and the words pour out, a story of a girl who had a twin who died in Mexico and how the other twin thinks of her. *(Una nina tiene una gemala que una vez se murio. Ahorra la gemela esta pensando en ella. Ella esta en el cemetaria.)* Sounding out words in Spanish helps Alma to write her story.

Marina, a 5-year-old Russian speaker, appreciates every chance she has to speak with Luba, the Russian aide and translator at her school. On her own, during writing workshop, Marina creates a little book with some writing in English and a few Cyrillic letters and words, like *CPMAS* for *Christmas.* She feels comfortable taking the risk of speaking to me and to others with a few words of English.

When Christina, a visiting teacher, spends the morning in the classroom, Marina discovers that Christina reads and writes Russian, and a quiet child becomes a chatterbox. Marina writes a story of her mom drying clothes in the *sun* [see "Marina's Writing"]. She uses English letters as she writes "CAOA," her invented spelling of the English word *sun.* For the Russian word sun (*conyue*), she uses "СОЦЕ," her invented spelling using Cyrillic letters. The Russian words for *clothes* and *drying the clothes* are written in Cyrillic, using invented spelling.

Marina's Writing

Because Christina was able to talk and write with Marina in both Russian and English, this encouraged Marina to speak and write in the two languages as well.

In the same class, Bennie makes similar strides in his writing. In the spring he reads his journal and explains his drawings in Cantonese when his mother comes for a parent conference. Bennie now speaks more frequently in English in class than he did earlier in the year and uses English phrases and gestures to tell about his writing. During the conference he expresses very complete thoughts about his writing, which we have never heard him do before.

The same week, he shares two pieces of writing with me: the first is a kind of picture story about spiders, birds, and his brother and sister [see "Bennie's Writing"]. In English letters he writes *Ming,* his Cantonese name, as well as *Bennie.* He includes his brother's English name, Alex, and a row of letters. On the same day, he writes a story in Chinese logographs—a skill we have never seen him use in class before [see "Bennie's Story"]. At the end of the day, I see him tuck this writing into his jacket pocket to take home and share with his family.

Bennie's Writing

Bennie's Story

Stories like these provide additional support for the research that shows dual language learners can write in both their home language and a second language without becoming confused. In a fascinating yearlong ethnography, Edelsky and Jilbert (1985) found that children learned both Spanish and English simultaneously without confusion, and they were able to differentiate between the two writing systems. In their Spanish invented spellings, the children used tildes (~) over the appropriate letters and never used the letter *k,* which Spanish speakers use only in foreign words. In any writing that the children read back in English, they omitted tildes and did use the letter *k.*

Reviewing Research Findings

Writing processes for young children are very similar across languages (Samway 2006). Even children whose first language is logographic, such Chinese and Korean, rather than alphabetic, like English or Spanish, invent spellings and writing symbols (Sebba 2007). When the two written language systems that children are learning are very different, children still draw on their knowledge of their home language as well as their growing understanding of English, testing out hypotheses just as they do in their oral language (Edelsky & Jilbert 1985).

Conclusion

All young children, whether English speaking or learning English as a second—or third!—language, blossom in environments that encourage genuine communication by whatever means work. Children need access to caring adults dedicated to making sense of what each child is trying to share through language, and they need to be a part of a learning community that encourages children's reliance on each other. Rather than sitting at a desk, focused on individual learning tasks, a workshop atmosphere encourages children to determine what tools, peers, and mentors will aid them in their quest to make meaning.

Nurturing Dual Language Learners' Writing Development

1. Look at each child as an individual. All writers are unique, and their writing development will reflect those idiosyncratic qualities. Get to know the children with whom you work, their interests, and their writing processes.

2. Encourage children to write and draw their stories right from the beginning, before they have mastered oral English.

3. Create opportunities for children to share writing with adults in the classroom and among their peers, young writers themselves.

4. Allow children the time and space they need to test out their hypotheses about written language.

5. Use each child's first language often and in as many different ways as possible in classroom activities.

6. Surround children with print in a range of languages and alphabetic and logographic systems.

References

Cunningham, A., & R. Shagoury. 2005. *Starting With Comprehension: Reading Strategies for the Youngest Learners.* Portland, ME: Stenhouse.

Edelsky, C., & K. Jilbert. 1985. "Bilingual Children and Writing: Lessons for All of Us." *Volta Review* 87 (5): 57–72.

Ernst, G., & K.J. Richard. 1995. "Reading and Writing Pathways to Conversation in the ESL Classroom." *The Reading Teacher* 48 (4): 320–26.

Freeman, Y.S., & D.E. Freeman. 2006. *Teaching Reading and Writing in Spanish and English in Bilingual and Dual Language Classrooms.* 2nd ed. Portsmouth, NH: Heinemann.

Freeman, D.E., & Y.S. Freeman. 2011. *Between Worlds: Access to Second Language Acquisition.* 3rd ed. Portsmouth, NH: Heinemann.

Garcia, O., & J. Kleifgen. 2010. *Educating Emergent Bilinguals: Policies, Programs, and Practices for English Language Learners.* New York: Teachers College Press.

Samway, K.D. 2006. *When English Language Learners Write: Connecting Research to Practice, K–8.* Portsmouth, NH: Heinemann.

Sebba, M. 2007. *Spelling and Society: The Culture and Politics of Orthography Around the World.* Cambridge, England: Cambridge University Press.

Shagoury, R. 2009. *Raising Writers: Understanding and Nurturing Young Children's Writing Development.* Boston: Allyn & Bacon.

Nell K. Duke

Let's Look in a Book! Using Nonfiction Reference Materials With Young Children

Dear Dr. Duke,

I think kids should read nonfiction books because they will make you smarter than you are.

Sincerely,
[First grade child]

I laughed when I first read this letter—but really, this child is right on target. Nonfiction resources contain so much more information than any one of us—child or teacher—can possibly hold. Much of the knowledge of our society, and of many of the societies that came before it, is accumulated in nonfiction texts. Nonfiction can answer many of the questions that we, and young children, have every day. And because the more you know, the more you realize you don't know, nonfiction raises new questions as well.

In this article I explain some of the potential benefits of using nonfiction reference materials with young children. I then provide ideas about ways to do this—everyday opportunities as well as more extensive projects in which to use a variety of nonfiction reference resources.

Think about how often you use nonfiction materials for reference. Perhaps you

• Check the weather forecast online, follow an evolving news story, find maps and directions, or gather teaching ideas

- Consult a cookbook or magazine for a recipe or general advice about how to use an ingredient
- Consult a guidebook to help you decide which sights to see when visiting another country
- Check the newspaper to learn about upcoming events in your community
- Reference an online dictionary or encyclopedia when you are unsure of a word, date, or concept or need to resolve a debate with a friend or loved one

Likely there are countless more ways you consult nonfiction materials on a regular basis.

You are not alone in your extensive use of nonfiction materials. In fact, studies of adult readers show that this is a common type of reading (e.g., White, Chen, & Forsyth 2010). Even those who may not regularly curl up with a novel or collection of poems do often read materials that are primarily nonfiction, such as periodicals, the most frequently read form of reading material, according to one study (White, Chen, & Forsyth 2010).

Amazingly, the nearly universal use of nonfiction materials for finding information seems to stop at many early childhood classroom doors. Early childhood classrooms seem to be the one place in which use of nonfiction reference materials—and reading of nonfiction in general—is rarely part of daily life (Pentimonti, Zucker, & Justice 2011), though this may change in K–3 due to expectations in the Common Core State Standards. The neglect of nonfiction could be justified if there were evidence that this kind of reading and these kinds of texts are inappropriate for children birth to 8. However, considerable research suggests that nonfiction genres—in particular informational text, on which most of the relevant research has been done—*are* appropriate for young children (see Duke 2003 for further discussion).

Why Use Nonfiction Reference Materials With Young Children?

There are some good reasons to include reading of nonfiction reference materials in early childhood settings.

> Dear Dr. Duke,
> I think that kids should read nonfiction books because they are smart they can do it I know they can they have the right . . .
>
> Sincerely,
> [First grade child]

Using nonfiction reference materials in the classroom allows children to see one important and common reason that people read. Given the importance of motivation to later literacy development, we want children to leave our programs feeling there are many important reasons to read. While reading stories for enjoyment is certainly one of them, reading to find answers to our questions, and to obtain information we want or need to know, is another.

Nell K. Duke, EdD, is a professor of literacy, language, and culture and a faculty affiliate for the combined program in education and psychology at the University of Michigan. Her coauthored books include *Reading and Writing Genre With Purpose in K to 8 Classrooms; Literacy and the Youngest Learner: Best Practices for Educators of Children From Birth to Five; and Beyond Bedtime Stories: A Parent's Guide to Promoting Reading, Writing, and Other Literacy Skills From Birth to 5.*

Author's Note: The author thanks Sue Sokolinski, a teacher who uses a great deal of nonfiction in her classroom, for providing the student letters that appear in this article.

For some children, reading nonfiction reference materials may be an especially compelling reason to read. We have all met a school-age child who pores over the encyclopedia, looking up one set of esoteric facts after another, or a preschooler who asks you to read the section about one or another dinosaur yet again. Some children seem to have a special interest in reading nonfiction (Mohr 2006; Chapman et al. 2007). Reading nonfiction for reference may help to engage these children.

Reading nonfiction reference materials helps deepen concepts of print and genre knowledge. I sometimes hear early childhood researchers or educators talk about reading a book from front to back as an important concept of print. While we do typically read stories all the way through from front to back, there are many kinds of texts that we don't read this way or that we don't read in their entirety. For example, with a parenting book like *What to Expect: The Toddler Years,* by Heidi E. Murkoff, Arlene Eisenberg, and Sandee Hathaway, I might first turn to the index in the back of the book, look for an entry related to the question I have, and then turn to the page or pages suggested. Or I might check the table of contents and from there go straight to the middle of the book, where the information I want is located. On the web—where I often turn for answers to questions—the concept of front to back hardly applies at all.

Reading nonfiction with young children helps them develop a more complex and accurate understanding of the different ways in which print works. In nonfiction-rich classrooms, I have seen young children skillfully navigate nonfiction in a variety of ways, even before they are reading conventionally. For example, children may flip through a text until they find a photo of what they are interested in or until they see a heading with the word or topic they were hoping to find. My daughter learned to look things up alphabetically when she was a kindergartner, motivated first by looking up friends' phone numbers for play dates. Selective and nonlinear reading is not out of reach for young children if they are given exposure to and opportunities for this kind of reading.

Reading nonfiction reference materials can also develop other kinds of knowledge, such as knowledge of language typical of one or more nonfiction genres (for example, language like "Some snakes eat rats" rather than "Sam the snake is eating a rat") and understanding of graphic devices like charts or diagrams often found in nonfiction texts (see Pappas 2006; Purcell-Gates, Duke, & Martineau 2007; Fingeret 2012). A variety of studies suggest that young children who are cared for in print-rich environments develop genre knowledge in the early years (Harste, Woodward, & Burke 1984; Donovan & Smolkin 2006). Using nonfiction reference materials may introduce children to genres they might not otherwise see in their homes or early childhood settings.

Reading nonfiction reference materials provides a forum for building computer literacy. For example, two Computer Practice and Programming Standards from the Computer Science Teachers Association (CSTA) for grades K–3 require that by the end of grade 3, children are able to "use technology resources to conduct age-appropriate research" and "use developmentally appropriate multimedia resources to support learning across the curriculum" (The CSTA Standards Task Force 2011, 14). These and similar standards can be addressed in part through reference activities, such as those outlined later in the article. There is an unprecedented amount of nonfiction material available; we should take advantage of this in our work with young children.

Dear Dr. Duke,

I think kids should read nonfiction books. Because kids learn about things that happen a long time ago. Also, they sometimes learn what's happening right now.

Sincerely,
[First grade child]

Reading nonfiction for reference provides another tool for developing comprehension and world knowledge. Many nonfiction texts convey information about the natural or social world. Young children can learn a great deal from these texts. Reference books like *How Things Work in the House,* by Lisa Campbell Ernst, help answer some of children's many "Why?" questions; globes, atlases, and maps help answer many questions about where things are; an Internet search can often help answer questions about who or what something is, and so on. Sometimes nonfiction reference materials can help children develop better understandings of things close to home, like how water gets out of their faucets; other times they help children learn about things very far away—the surface of the moon, the depths of the ocean—things they may never experience firsthand.

Many educators worry that we are not doing enough to build children's world knowledge—their knowledge base in science, social studies, health, history, and so on (e.g., Neuman 2006). With nonfiction texts used for reference, you can help develop both literacy skills and world knowledge (though firsthand experiences as a means of developing world knowledge are also key).

Ideas for Using Nonfiction Reference Materials With Young Children

There are many ways you can work reading nonfiction reference materials into everyday activities in the classroom. Here are a few.

When questions arise, say, "Let's look in a book" (or on the computer). A child asks, "What is a pulley?" Two children are arguing about whether an animal picture shows an alligator or a crocodile. A visitor explains she has just returned from Indonesia—"Indo-where?" the children ask.

Questions constantly come up in early childhood settings, especially in settings in which asking questions is encouraged. You can take these opportunities to illustrate how nonfiction texts can often answer our questions. Open the dictionary for an explanation and picture of a pulley. Consult an encyclopedia to find differences between alligators and crocodiles (there are encyclopedias designed especially for children, such as *First Animal Encyclopedia* [DK Publishing], which has an entry on this very topic). A map, globe, or atlas will help children locate Indonesia.

Before a field trip, look up directions and a map to the location on the Internet. If applicable, visit the location's website or look up other information related to the trip. For example, if it is a trip to the zoo, read about a special exhibit or about an animal the children are especially eager to see.

Look up phone numbers and addresses for inquiries, thank-you notes, and other communications. Model for children, or have them work with you or on their own, looking for information they need to send cards, letters, emails, or other correspondence. Children are often keen to share what they have drawn and/or written, and will work hard to get the information they need to do so.

Check the weather in a newspaper or online. A persistent question for early childhood educators and children is what the weather is or will be to determine whether an excursion is possible, whether children will need their coats, or whether they can go outside at all. Help children learn how to get this information from a website, newspaper, or a weather channel on TV. Children will quickly come to recognize key words and symbols that represent different weather types.

Dear Dr. Duke,

I thike that kids shod rede noficshin books because pepol shod lern ubowt things that pepol never learnd ubowt.

Sincerely,
[First grade child]

Follow current events. The weather report isn't the only timely information to share with children. Checking on current events via the Internet, newspapers, or magazines can be a valuable learning opportunity. Children may become engaged in a particular story, such as preparation for the Olympic games, the construction of a new building, or the progress of a space mission, and want to follow it as it unfolds. Or you might engage children in flipping through a periodical, including one designed for children, such as *National Geographic Young Explorer,* scanning for an article of interest.

Make use of field guides. Children are often interested in identifying things in nature—birds, trees or leaves, insects, and more. Having field guides available helps with this. Children can use adult field guides, with a lot of teacher support, or you can look for field guides or field-guide-like texts that are designed for young children, such as *Autumn Leaves,* by Ken Robbins, or *Bugs A to Z,* by Caroline Lawton.

Dear Dr. Duke,

Kids should read nonfiction books in first grade because if you like football for example if you just read storys. you couldn't find out about football.

Sincerely,
[First grade child]

Explore record books. Many children are fascinated by the concept of records— How tall is the tallest person in the world? What is the largest animal? Who was the first person to fly around the world? Record books, many of which can be made accessible for young children, provide answers to lots of such questions. There are also picture books that focus on records within a specific category, such as *The Animal Book: A Collection of the Fastest, Fiercest, Toughest, Cleverest, Shyest—and Most Surprising—Animals on Earth,* by Steve Jenkins.

Be on the lookout for reference materials that will be popular with individuals in your group. One child may find sports most fascinating; for another, it may be trains or horses or princesses. There are reference materials available on all of these topics, and more. If you don't have them in your collection, consider borrowing them from the library or purchasing them with book club dividends. Some teachers suggest that parents can donate a book, rather than sweets, when a child's birthday comes around. If you do this, you might suggest that the parent look for a nonfiction book on a topic of passionate interest to the child.

Have ample books available for reference during themes and units. Whatever the focus of your instruction, don't be afraid to involve and refer to books or other resources as well as engage children in firsthand experiences. Research suggests that the combination of both texts and firsthand experiences leads to greater content learning than firsthand experiences alone (Cervetti et al. 2012).

A Caution

Sum tim they are bad sum tim they are good.
[First grade child]

Finally, a warning about using nonfiction materials for reference: it is important to remember, and to help children learn early on, that just because something is published does not mean it is true. Some nonfiction materials, particularly on the Internet, are riddled with factual errors. And often there are different legitimate opinions about an issue—such as why dinosaurs became extinct—all of which should be represented. Indeed, yet another benefit of reading nonfiction materials for reference with young children is the opportunity to put children on the road toward critical reading as they gather information from multiple sources.

So remember: Don't forget the nonfiction. As a wise first-grader once told me, "It will make you smarter than you are!"

Nonfiction and Class Projects

Teachers can involve students in more extensive projects that include using nonfiction materials for reference. For example, my colleagues and I have worked with first grade teachers to involve children in writing booklets related to food. The books were then displayed at a local restaurant. Children used nonfiction reference materials to investigate where particular foods are made, how popular they are, and their nutritional value, along with other information. Moreover, we found when teachers engage children in projects like these the children develop stronger informational writing skills than children who experience more traditional writers' workshop experiences. For descriptions of projects like this, please see Duke, Caughlan, Juzwik, and Martin (2012).

References

Cervetti, G.N., J. Barber, R. Dorph, P.D. Pearson, & P.G. Goldschmidt. 2012. "The Impact of an Integrated Approach to Science and Literacy in Elementary School Classrooms." *Journal of Research in Science Teaching* 49: 631–58.

Chapman, M., M. Filipenko, M. McTavish, & J. Shapiro. 2007. "First Graders' Preferences for Narrative and/or Information Books and Perceptions of Other Boys' and Girls' Book Preferences." *Canadian Journal of Education* 30: 531–53. www.files.eric.ed.gov/fulltext/EJ780784.pdf.

The CSTA Standards Task Force. 2011. *CSTA K–12 Computer Science Standards.* Rev. New York: Computer Science Teachers Association (CSTA) and Association for Computing Machinery (ACM).

Donovan, C.A., & L.B. Smolkin. 2006. "Children's Understanding of Genre and Writing Development." In *Handbook of Writing Research,* eds. C.A. MacArthur, S. Graham, & J. Fitzgerald, 131–43. New York: Guilford Press.

Duke, N.K. 2003. "Reading to Learn From the Very Beginning: Information Books in Early Childhood." *Young Children* 58 (3): 14–20.

Duke, N.K., S. Caughlan, M.M. Juzwik, & N.M. Martin. 2012. *Reading and Writing Genre With Purpose in K–8 Classrooms.* Portsmouth, NH: Heinemann.

Fingeret, L. 2012. "Graphics in Children's Informational Texts: A Content Analysis." PhD diss., Michigan State University.

Harste, J.C., V.A. Woodward, & C. Burke. 1984. *Language Stories and Literacy Lessons.* Portsmouth, NH: Heinemann.

Mohr, K.A.J. 2006. "Children's Choices for Recreational Reading: A Three-Part Investigation of Selection Preferences, Rationales, and Processes." *Journal of Literacy Research* 38 (1): 81–104.

Neuman, S.B. 2006. "The Knowledge Gap: Implications for Early Education." In *Handbook of Early Literacy Research, Vol. 2,* eds. D.K. Dickinson & S.B. Neuman, 29–40. New York: Guilford.

Pappas, C.C. 2006. "The Information Book Genre: Its Role in Integrated Science Literacy Research and Practice." *Reading Research Quarterly* 41 (2): 226–50.

Pentimonti, J.M., T.A. Zucker, & L.M Justice. 2011. "What Are Preschool Teachers Reading in Their Classrooms?" *Reading Psychology* 32: 197–236. doi: 10.1080/02702711003604484.

Purcell-Gates, V., N.K. Duke, & J.A. Martineau. 2007. "Learning to Read and Write Genre-Specific Text: Roles of Authentic Experience and Explicit Teaching." *Reading Research Quarterly* 42 (1): 8–45.

White, S., J. Chen, & B. Forsyth. 2010. "Reading-Related Literacy Activities of American Adults: Time Spent, Task Types, and Cognitive Skills Used." *Journal of Literacy Research* 42: 276–307. doi: 10.1080/1086296X.2010.503552.

Other Resources

In addition to the children's books mentioned in the article, here are a few suggestions for starting the nonfiction library in the classroom. Magazine articles may inspire children to use nonfiction materials to find out more.

Children's Magazines

chickaDEE. Online: www.owlkids.com/magazines/chickadee

Click. www.cricketmag.com/ProductDetail.asp?pid=6

National Geographic Kids. www.kids.nationalgeographic.com

National Geographic Little Kids. www.littlekids.national geographic.com/littlekids

National Geographic Young Explorer. www.ngexplorer.cengage.com/ngyoungexplorer/

Ranger Rick Jr. www.nwf.org/Kids/Ranger-Rick-Jr.aspx

Zoobooks. www.zoobooks.com

My Big World. http://classroommagazines.scholastic.com/products/my-big-world

Let's Find Out. http://classroommagazines.scholastic.com/products/let-s-find-out

Jane A. Hansen

First Grade Writers Revisit Their Work

The young children in this article are readers and writers who revisit their work. They care enough to want it to be right. As with adults, deciding whether to reread or revise isn't an issue; it's just what you do. Even grown-ups may read their favorite books over and over, and good writers revise their work again and again.

Horn and Giacobbe (2007) point out children's natural revisions to their speech as they use language with others, and the revisions they make to their drawings. A natural extension of these revisions is the changes young writers intentionally make to their written words.

Zinsser (2006) addresses adults in his well-known guide to nonfiction writing, but basic writing principles hold true for children too. Zinsser pronounces rewriting to be the "essence of writing well; it's where the game is won or lost" (83). He shows how one sentence promises the next. Even young children, when they reread their drafts, can sense when a piece of needed information is absent.

In relation to nonfiction writing and reading, Phillips (2009) observed young children presenting their content in the formats they encountered in books during the research phase of their writing. For example, depending on what they had seen in the books, they would display their illustrations at the top of a page of writing, or at the bottom, or place the illustrations and text side by side.

In a Virginia first grade classroom, I too encountered motivated writers and readers. In the narrative that follows, I recount what children do when they revisit their writing about science and literature and review collections of their work.

A Classroom of Writers

The first-graders discussed here were in Elaine O'Connor's classroom at Clark Elementary School in Charlottesville. Clark is a Title I school with a student body that is 64 percent African American, 24 percent White, 7 percent Hispanic, and 5 percent other ethnicities. Eighty percent of the school's students receive a free or discounted lunch—the highest percentage in the Charlottesville City Schools.

Children came to Elaine's classroom with varied histories as writers. Some had attended a kindergarten in which they wrote every day, and others, as far as we knew, had not written at all. Their progress was impressive.

The Writers' Workshop

Every Tuesday and Thursday I participated in the writers' workshop in Elaine's classroom as a researcher who wanted to know what young writers do. I was present for the entire 45-minute workshop, and recorded the children's comments as they interacted with each other and with Elaine. I also conferred with them and photocopied samples of their work. Once each week, Elaine and I met to discuss the children's writing development; these conversations helped further my understanding of their intentions as writers.

The children wrote on Mondays and Wednesdays on whatever topics they wished, and on Tuesdays and Thursdays they usually wrote on a topic related to a unit of study the class was pursuing. Over the course of the year, the children engaged in six kinds of writing experiences during the days I was there. They wrote about math, science, and social studies, and they wrote personal narratives, self-evaluations, and responses to literature. Of these, I focus in this article on assignments given in the first three months of school: writing about science, responses to literature, and self-evaluations.

The schedule generally began with the children gathered in a cluster on the floor for a brief lesson by Elaine. Sometimes she introduced a new writing assignment that fit with a unit of study; during other sessions she invited the children to work on a draft begun previously.

Next the children went to their tables to write. There were four tables, with the children carefully placed by Elaine so that each table included children with differing strengths as writers. The children typically worked on a piece of writing for more than one session.

While the children wrote, they chattered. They asked and answered each others' questions, offered unsolicited advice (often appreciated and sometimes not), argued about whether eagles glide with their wings outstretched or tight to their bodies, and marveled at each others' illustrations. Their talk contributed greatly to their feeling of community, a highly necessary ingredient for a classroom of

Jane A. Hansen, PhD, is professor emerita in the Curry School of Education at the University of Virginia in Charlottesville. She has conducted research in New Hampshire and Virginia on the relationships between writing and reading and on children as writers across the curriculum.

Children's work samples courtesy of the author.

Author's Note: I want to thank Elaine O'Connor for welcoming me into the writers' workshops in her classroom.

Bryantae's World

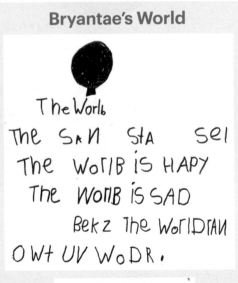

The Worlb
The SuN STa seL
The WorlB iS HAPY
The WonB iS SAD
Bekz The WorlDrAN
O Wt UV WoDR.

The World
The sun stays still.
The world is happy.
The world is sad
because the world ran
out of water.

writers. The children felt comfortable trying out new processes, which was important for them in intentionally becoming better writers.

During this writing time Elaine, the full-time instructional aide Denise Mowry, and I conferred with the children. Elaine and Denise moved from table to table, from child to child. I sat in place at one table, a different one each time I visited, because, for my research, it was useful to know as much as possible about the processes that surrounded the children's drafts at a particular time.

We three adults focused on content, the information the children needed when they wrote on topics across the curriculum. When children had written everything they wanted to say about a topic, we pointed out one thing (or more) to each child in the realm of mechanics. It might have been the need for a capital letter on a name or the need for a question mark instead of a period—something that could be easily fixed. The child corrected this, and the draft was finished, at least for the time being. The children usually revisited their drafts after several days passed. Elaine frequently observed the children making voluntary revisions on their writing drafts to improve them; however, she did not require revisions. Graves (2003) finds this flexibility important. He cautions teachers not to turn revision into orthodoxy; there should be no rigid writing process for all children to follow. Typically, at the end of each writers' workshop, two of the children read their drafts to the class to celebrate their work.

Engaged Scientists Revisit Their Writing

For several days Elaine used the globe and nonfiction literature to discuss the tilt of Earth and how it contributed to changes in our weather during the fall. On a Tuesday, she invited the children to write about something they'd learned about fall.

On Thursday Elaine asked Bryantae and Casey if they wanted to read their drafts aloud to the class. Bryantae read first (see "Bryantae's World," p. 65). Notice her concern about water. All the children were very aware of the drought in the Charlottesville area at the time; the school's water faucets had been turned off, and a sanitizing solution had been provided for hand washing.

The children listened for what they could learn from Bryantae and asked questions to find out more—important tasks in writing across the curriculum. Jeremiah picked up on the line "The world ran out of water," and several children commented on the drought until one changed the subject by saying, "I learned that the world is happy." Another child wondered why, and Bryantae wasn't sure how to answer that. Elaine said, "Maybe Bryantae will think about it and add that new information today." The children understood: Bryantae didn't have to add anything to her draft, but maybe she would.

Next Casey read her draft (see "Casey's World"). In the class conversation that followed, one child repeated what he learned: "We can't feel the world going around." Another said, "I learned that it takes one day to go around the sun." Elaine, knowing

Casey's World

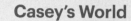

The world turns away
from the sun and
the sun stays still
and we cannot
feel it. The world goes around the
sun. It takes one day. I know how the
world goes on its axis. By Casey

that these were difficult concepts for the beginning of first grade, carefully reviewed the Earth's rotation on its axis and its orbit around the sun. The children then went off to write, free to either start a new draft or work on a previous one.

Bryantae chose to revisit her draft and inserted two pieces of information: after the line [The sun stays still], she wrote But The WorD seN [but the world spins], and after [The world is happy], she added Bekes it is koD [because it is cold].

Casey's draft and the conversation about the Earth spinning prompted Bryantae to clarify her thinking and then to wonder about what might make the world happy. (Evidently, if the world is going to become colder each fall, it must like that!)

However skilled they may be, it is often difficult for young writers to know what they don't know. Sometimes an honest misunderstanding on the part of a classmate leads a writer to change a few words, as Bryantae did. When a writer cares about her writing, becomes aware of a gap, and knows how to fill it in, she does so.

Engaged Readers Revisit Their Writing and Reading

At the start of the year Elaine read several Clifford books (the series by Norman Bridwell). On September 19 she asked the children to write about the big red dog. Samantha, her pony-tail swinging from side to side, headed for her table. She loved Clifford and quickly drew him (see "Samantha's Clifford 1") and wrote CLeFRd big over his head. She added Red, and a boy noticed. He pointed on his draft to a lowercase *r* and told Samantha to write hers that way. Ignoring him, Samantha turned to me and asked, "How do you spell *watchdog*?" I helped her stretch the word out. As she listened to herself sound it out, she wrote woJdog. Samantha read the sentence aloud to me— "Clifford big red is watchdog"—and I saw a bit of a cloud creep over her face. I said nothing, and neither did Samantha, but she knew something sounded wrong. After reading the sentence again, to herself, she erased Red and in its place wrote He.

Samantha read her revision to me—"Clifford big He is watchdog"—and we talked about Clifford as a watchdog. Just as I was about to say something about the missing words in her writing, Samantha got up, walked to the work box (a large, decorated cardboard box), and filed her work. She got a new sheet of paper to begin a draft about something entirely different. She didn't appear to be as excited as she had been at the beginning of writing class, and I got the definite impression that an offer to help her clarify her writing would have been, at this point, pushing too hard. Samantha had shown me that she knew how to clarify her writing, and I knew the classroom routine of returning to one's work, if a writer so desired, was an option the

Samantha's Clifford 1

Clifford big.
He is watchdog.

Samantha's Clifford 2

Clifford is a good watch dog. He can watch very good. He can jump high. He can't fit in a house.

Samantha's Clifford 3

Clifford When he was a
baby he was a tenny
its baby that clifford mom
hab and Emily Elizabeth
Wood nove let any tag
hap in to Clifford

Clifford

When he was a
baby he was a teeny
itsy baby that Clifford's mom
had and Emily Elizabeth
would not have let anything
happen to Clifford.

children often chose. I would find out during my future visits whether Samantha would decide to revise this writing on Clifford.

After writers' workshop Elaine and I looked at the children's work, and she noticed the shortness of many of the drafts. She decided it was time to nudge the class. She suspected the children knew much more about Clifford than they had written. For Thursday's mini-lesson, Elaine wrote a draft about Clifford in which she included several pieces of information. The children became excited. Collectively, they revealed even more details about the big dog. Energized and informed, they went off to write.

For the moment, though, Samantha seemed to have lost interest in Clifford. She wrote about something else. It was not until September 24 that she returned to Clifford (see "Samantha's Clifford 2," p. 67).

I was amazed by Samantha's progress as a writer in only one week. It always impresses me how quickly young children progress when they write every day, receive lots of support, and are motivated to learn and write.

Throughout the fall and early spring, Elaine occasionally reread a Clifford book, and Samantha sometimes perused one on her own or with a friend. Her interest in Clifford renewed in the spring when she made a great discovery: she could read his books, in part, by herself! Samantha became determined to learn to read them, and one day appeared to understand an important, personal characteristic of Clifford's best friend, Emily Elizabeth. She quickly made a journal entry (see "Samantha's Clifford 3").

Samantha, writing with increasing fluency, understood the Clifford books at a deeper level than she had earlier in the year. By revisiting Clifford over several months, Samantha gained an appreciation for these classic stories and knew she was becoming a reader.

Revisiting both reading and writing helps children hear themselves gradually become able to read beloved books and see their writing progress. They start to value their own growth over time.

Engaged Writers Revisit Their Accomplishments

On September 24 Elaine asked the children to retrieve all their drafts from the work box and to study their collections. They were to observe their changes, think about what they had learned, and consider what they might do to grow as writers.

I sat on the carpet with Alexis. She studied her writing seriously, carefully reviewing and then turning over each draft so the print was out of view. As Alexis turned over the last one, I assumed she would go through them again and talk about what she had learned. Instead, she placed them back in her folder, looked at me, and said, "I can't read any of them."

Before I could respond, Alexis walked away, returned with a new sheet of paper, and announced, "I'm going to write something I can read." She thought for a while and decided to write about school the day before, when the children ate lunch in their classroom. As she reached for her pencil, I turned my attention elsewhere.

After a few minutes I saw that Alexis had written something but then crossed it out. She explained, "I made a new decision. I'm writing to Miss Mowry." (Denise had celebrated her birthday the previous day, and the children had all created cards for her.) I thought, "How wise this young child is. If a writer wants to write something that is readable, a letter is a sound choice. The other person has to be able to read it."

Todd, sitting on Alexis's right, leaned over to help her get started with her note. A little later, I saw that Alexis had a good start, but I also noticed that two of the words were in Todd's handwriting. I told him it was wonderful for him to help Alexis figure out her letters and sounds but, I added, she should be the only one to write on her paper. "We don't write on our friend's drawings, and we don't write on their writing. We just don't write on others' works."

I listened while Alexis stretched the sounds in the next word, letter by letter, then wrote B R D A. She paused for what felt to me like a long time, and I thought I should bring her back to task. I asked her what she would write next. She said, "One day can you eat lunch with me."

I turned my attention to other children, and when I got back to Alexis, I saw that she had written 1DCE WME. Alexis pointed to each letter and began to read, "One day can you," then hesitated before squeezing a U between the C and E. Her question read: "One day can you eat with me?" She knew what she was going to write next, she said: "I love you, Miss Mowry." At the end of class, I saw her completed note (see "Alexis's Letter").

Alexis beamed, proud of her letter. She had written it carefully and could read it; therefore, Miss Mowry would surely be able to do likewise! Alexis's decision to write to Miss Mowry appeared to have been a good one. She knew that by slowing down and listening for each word and sound, she could write text that was more readable.

When children write about something they care about, they not only want to be able to read it, they also want it to sound right. This note was important to Alexis; she loved Miss Mowry. Our ultimate goal when we teach young writers is for them to bring their strong, young voices into print (Cappello 2006), and Alexis's letter did just that.

Alexis's Letter

A DRA MAiN
HON is YOOR BRDA IDCE WME
i LUM iS MARE
F AlExis

Dear Miss Mowry
How is your birthday?
One day can you eat with me?
I love you, Miss Mowry.
Alexis

Quoshad's Dad

QUOSHAd
I Play wof mi dod

Learning About the Parallel Between Words and Illustrations

In November, when the children again studied their collections, Elaine suggested, "Choose three pieces you think are interesting. Be able to explain why you chose them. Then think of what you want to do so you'll grow as a writer. You can work on a draft in your folder or start a new one."

I sat on the carpet with Quoshad, who was thumbing through his drafts. Quoshad could not read most of them, but he stopped at a drawing and said, "This is me playing with my dad. Oh! I forgot the steps!" He immediately drew in steps to the second floor, where he and his father played computer games. He then said, "This needs a title!" and added words (see "Quoshad's Dad").

As he continued to study his collection, Quoshad stopped at a long draft written on the day Elaine had asked the class to write about fall. I had joined Quoshad's table that day, and he had immediately begun to draw pumpkins. Looking around the table, however, he had noticed that most of the children were writing about the world. He had decided to do likewise, and after changing one of his orange pumpkins to a blue Earth, he had begun writing.

Quoshad's Evolving World

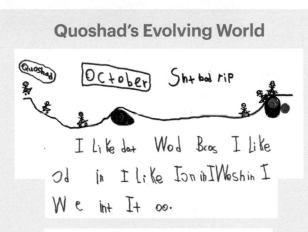

Quoshad   October   Sht bod rip

I li ke dot Wod Beas I like
ɔd in I li ke Iɔn in IWeshin I
We int It oo.

Skateboard Ramp

I like the world because I like
candy and I like ice cream
and I will share and I
won't eat it all.

Quoshad Begins a New Text

THe Sht bod man

The Skateboard Man

Two days later, Quoshad drew a skateboard ramp on top of the world and added children at play. Later, as he shared that draft from his collection with me, he proceeded to bring the skateboarders to life. "This one is jumping up, way up!" He drew one boy flying off the center hump. "Nooo! He falls!" and Quoshad erased him. In video fashion, Quoshad described the various jumps and twists of his characters, moving them about and adding and erasing as fast as he talked. He then said, "This needs a title!" and wrote Sht bod rip [Skateboard Ramp] (see "Quoshad's Evolving World").

Without a word, Quoshad fetched a new sheet of paper. "This goes here," he said as he placed the blank sheet over the bottom half of the draft, covering the words about the world, candy, and ice cream. He wrote The Sht bod man [The Skateboard Man] (see "Quoshad Begins a New Text").

Upon studying his body of work, Quoshad figured out the need to match text and pictures. He wrote words to match his illustration, and his new composition became a singular entity. This began Quoshad's new journey as a writer. Revisiting his collection of drafts led him to see himself as someone who intentionally became a better writer as the months passed.

Elaine wanted the children to see themselves as writers, taking responsibility for their growth (Hansen et al. 2010). It was obvious that this was happening.

Conclusion

Wohlwend (2009) writes about assessment in classrooms of young writers. Revision is the ultimate assessment for them, as it is for all writers. Young children evaluate their own work as they determine whether their words and messages are clear. They read their writing to others, share it with the teacher, compare it with other pieces of writing, and change it if they are not pleased. The children in Elaine's class did this. They gradually understood the Earth and Clifford, even the focusing power of a title.

As young writers develop a vision of what they can do, they see new opportunities. Excitement leads them to reenvision possibilities (Ray 2004). When children see their drafts as invitations to play, they often totally remove parts and transform drafts into pieces of writing with far more zest than they originally possessed.

Just as children naturally rework playdough, they naturally rework their writing. Revising is what they do (Solley 2005); a crayon can change a bear into an alien at will. Children use writing as a flexible, recursive process before they have ever heard of revision.

Young writers want their work to look and sound a certain way. Elaine's motivated children regularly wrote across the curriculum and frequently revisited their work. As with adult readers and writers, whether to reread or revise isn't an issue. It's what writers who care do.

References

Cappello, M. 2006. "Under Construction: Voice and Identity Development in Writing Workshop." *Language Arts* 83 (6): 482–91.

Graves, D.H. 2003. "Preface." In *Writing: Teachers and Children at Work,* 20th anniversary ed., vii–xv. Portsmouth, NH: Heinemann.

Hansen, J., R. Davis, J. Evertson, T. Freeman, D. Suskind, & H. Tower. 2010. *The PreK–2 Writing Classroom: Growing Confident Writers.* New York: Scholastic.

Horn, M., & M.E. Giacobbe. 2007. *Talking, Drawing, Writing: Lessons for Our Youngest Writers.* Portland, ME: Stenhouse.

Phillips, H. 2009. "Emerging Inquiry: Using Nonfiction to Guide Student Research." *Social Studies and the Young Learner* 22 (1): 23–26.

Ray, K.W., With L.B. Cleaveland. 2004. *About the Authors: Writing Workshop With Our Youngest Writers.* Portsmouth, NH: Heinemann.

Solley, B.A. 2005. *When Poverty's Children Write: Celebrating Strengths, Transforming Lives.* Portsmouth, NH: Heinemann.

Wohlwend, K.E. 2009. "Dilemmas and Discourses of Learning to Write: Assessment as a Contested Site." *Language Arts* 86 (5): 341–51.

Zinsser, W. 2006. *On Writing Well: The Classic Guide to Writing Nonfiction.* 30th anniversary ed. New York: HarperCollins.

Charles A. Elster

"Snow on My Eyelashes"—Language Awareness Through Age-Appropriate Poetry Experiences

Rhymes and poems can be a natural starting point for young children as they experience the world and learn to understand spoken, written, and visual languages. Poetry contains highly patterned, predictable language that has unique potential to promote memorable and pleasurable experiences in preschool, kindergarten, and primary classrooms. Rather than using language just to transmit a message, poetic devices like sound play, figurative meaning, ambiguous pronoun references, unusual sentence structures, and the graphic pattern of short lines on the page, use language to slow down the reading process and invite readers to pay attention to the words themselves (see "About Poetry," p. 74).

As children gain literacy skills in the primary grades, they build on knowledge of spoken language, which is invisible and temporary, to explore written language, which is visible and more permanent. Age-appropriate experiences with poetry can increase young children's attention to the many possible uses and techniques of language. Awareness of language is a key to literacy learning, but an overemphasis on one aspect of language awareness—

phonemic awareness—sometimes limits educators' views of the broader picture. In this article I explore the value of poetry experiences for promoting young children's language awareness, with phonemic awareness as one part of that learning process, and I share two teachers' classroom approaches.

From Phonemic Awareness to Language Awareness

Phonemic awareness is the understanding that spoken words can be divided into discrete sounds called phonemes (for example, *ship* = /sh//i//p/) (see Yopp & Yopp 2009). It is a key component in connecting written letters and their sounds. This ability supports young children as they learn to read and write.

But phonemic awareness alone is not sufficient to allow children to become proficient readers and writers. *Language awareness* is the broader understanding that (1) language is composed of words, sentences, and larger units that serve important personal, social, and academic functions; (2) words are composed of sounds, syllables, and letters; (3) words have multiple meanings, depending on where they are used; and (4) language is an interesting and important subject of study. As children learn about written language and its uses and forms, shared reading of various genres with parents, teachers, and others serves as the foundation for their own independent reading. In learning to read and write, children learn to orchestrate and balance four systems related to language use: the connection between letters and sounds (graphophonological system), expected sentence structures (syntax), word meanings (semantics), and real-life language uses (pragmatics). And as the pioneer teacher-researcher Don Holdaway (1979) stressed, familiar, predictable, pleasurable texts are important scaffolds for emerging readers and writers.

Reading, rereading, performing, and discussing poetry promotes young readers' and writers' language awareness. On the phonological (sound) level, poetry includes many types of sound repetition: rhyme, alliteration, assonance (see "Poetry Terms"). On the syntactic level, poetry provides sentence frames and refrains. It can contain nonstandard grammar ("I ain't never gonna spend it"). It also provides the challenge of unfamiliar syntax, such as subject–verb reversal ("falls a raindrop") and verb ellipsis ("sunshine fading"). On the semantic level, poetry offers a rich repertoire of vocabulary, especially words related to the senses, and patterns of words that "go together" as opposites, sequences, cause–effect, part–whole, and other relationships. On the pragmatic level, poems fulfill functions of pleasure and social bonding as well as language play.

Poetry Terms

Alliteration: Repetition of one or more initial sounds in words (*where the Grickle Grass grows*).

Assonance: Repetition of vowel sounds that falls short of rhyme (*lay them straight*).

Couplet: A pair of adjacent rhyming lines.

Line: A spoken or written unit consisting of a breath unit and/or regular patterns of beats, rhyme, or other sound play.

Poetry: Language that calls attention to itself as language in order to be entertaining or memorable; often contains structural repetition, sound play, bold images, and figurative language.

Refrain: A repeated line or phrase (. . . *I like best*).

Rhyme: Repetition of sounds at the end of syllables (*One, two/buckle my shoe*).

Rhyme pattern: Repetition of end-rhymes in stanzas.

Rhythm, Beat, Meter: All refer to patterns of stressed and unstressed syllables in a line (e.g., *Snow in the east/snow in the west* are two-beat lines).

Sound play: The use of sounds within words to organize the poem and affect the reader.

Stanza: A group of lines separated from others by a line space.

Structural repetition: Patterns that organize poems.

Charles A. Elster, PhD, is a professor in the School of Education at Sonoma State University in Rohnert Park, California, where he teaches courses in child development, literacy, and children's literature. Charles is interested in new forms of literature for children.

About Poetry

Before writing was invented, poetry was literature. Because poetry was an orally transmitted literature, its creators sought to maximize memorization and oral performance.

Poetic resources include sound effects (rhythm, rhyme, alliteration, and others), unusual sentence patterns, and multiple word meanings, including secondary meanings, metaphor, personification, and other effects. Poems often contain striking imagery, storytelling, and structural repetition at many levels. Written poems have a graphic layout of words, lines, and stanzas that accentuate their formal features. Poets use techniques like these to draw the attention of readers, writers, listeners, and speakers beyond the message that language conveys to the language itself.

As memorable language, poetry is ideal for transmitting cultural knowledge. Proverbs, another form of oral folklore, use poetic resources like rhyme, alliteration, and semantic contrast to be memorable: "Haste makes waste," "Look before you leap," "Don't make a mountain out of a molehill." Rhymes, songs, lullabies, and poems have always existed in all cultures alongside prose stories, to transmit cultural knowledge and to provide shared words that can be spoken on important occasions.

Poetry is not a genre, like stories or informational texts, but a mode of language that contrasts with everyday prose because it has a regular beat or other formal organizing pattern. This pattern augments the message that the words convey. Poems may tell stories or impart information. Poetry is rooted in the rhythmic movements of the breath and the body in ways that ordinary prose is not. The most often-read poems today are usually short and lyrical, conveying human experience in condensed or playful language; but longer, narrative, informational, and hybrid poems are becoming more plentiful (see "Poems to Share With Young Children," p. 80).

The personal, lyrical voice of poetry is at the opposite end of the spectrum from the impersonal, logical voice of prose essays. Because poetry is a condensed language of image and sound pattern, a large part of the aesthetic pleasure of poetry, like that of a play or a song, is in its performance. Poems and rhymes are a good starting point for young children who are moving from unconscious to conscious understandings of language, from using language as a tool to talk about the world to language as an object of attention and study in its own right. Poetry can satisfy a young child's search for pleasure, pattern recognition, and play, and the opportunity to take part in poetry performance makes literature and learning personal and concrete.

How Teachers Share Poems With Young Children

There has been recent interest in using poetry as a vehicle for helping struggling readers (Rasinski & Zimmerman 2013) and for promoting reading fluency through repeated readings (Faver 2008). Although its broader value has been studied occasionally (Gill 2007), its importance in language and literacy development has received little recent attention, compared to the attention given to other types of text. For example, the Common Core State Standards for English Language Arts puts more emphasis on informational text than on poetry (NGACBP & CCSSO 2010).

Many accounts of poetry in primary grade classrooms (e.g., Kovalcik & Certo 2007; McNair 2012) show teachers leading a variety of activities, from the intuitive to the analytical, from nurturing aesthetic sensitivity to exploring poetic techniques. Typical activities involve encouraging children to listen to, recite, read, and write poems; to respond through talk and visual arts; and to explore thematic connections.

A colleague and I studied the literature practices of 10 veteran K–2 teachers in several midwestern schools. All of the teachers routinely used literature in the classroom and received no other instructions than to share poems with the children as they normally would. We found that teachers read poems aloud to their students differently than they did stories: more slowly and with more expression, often rereading poems in a single sitting and encouraging children to participate in reading along (Elster & Hanauer 2002). Teachers seemed to naturally emphasize the enjoyment of poetry as language and performance.

Some teachers in our study were especially strong at using poetry experiences to build children's awareness of language. In the classroom dialogues that follow, Mr. Porter reads Eve Merriam's poem "Snow in the East" with his first grade class, and Mrs. Light discusses

Merriam's "You Be Saucer" with her second grade class—both poems from Merriam's *You Be Good and I'll Be Night.*

Mr. Porter's Poetry Reading

"Snow in the East" is a 20-line lyric of five stanzas with two-beat lines, an *abcb* rhyme pattern, and a refrain of "I like best." As the transcript of his poetry reading shows, Mr. Porter engaged children in a pointing routine during his first reading, allowing them to participate nonverbally in a fast-paced reading of the poem even before they had learned the words. (Spoken words and syllables that are italicized in the transcript indicate emphasis by the speaker.)

Mr. Porter: Let's do a real short one in here *(turns the pages of the book)* that's a little bit about the weather. Remember some of the songs we learned so far? "This land is *your* land, this land is *my* land, from . . . "

Children: "Cali*for*nia"

Mr. P: "to the . . . "

Children: "New York *is*land."

Mr. P: Okay, now. That's as far as we need to go. Do you remember which way we point? Which way do we point for California?

Children: *(point to a sign saying West, posted on the appropriate wall)*

Mr. P: Okay, California's *that* way *(points)*. Way out *west.*

Children: West.

Mr. P: Which way do we point for New York?

Jimmy: East.

Children: *(point to the East sign posted on the eastern wall)*

Mr. P: That's *that* way *(points)*. That's way out *east.* We're in the middle. Now, you're going to need to know those directions, because you're going to have to point in this poem. Let's do the first part. If I say, "Snow in the *east,*" where would you point?

Children: *(point in different directions)*

Mr. P: Joey's got it right. "Snow in the *west,* . . ."

Children: *(point in different directions)*

Mr. P: That's *that* way *(points toward the west)*. Now, it's nice to have snow in the east and snow in the west, because people like to go skiing. But this is going to tell us where *this* little girl likes to have snowflakes *(shows the picture)*. "Snow in the *east,* . . ."

Children: *(point)*

Mr. P: "Snow in the *west,* . . ."

Children: *(point)*

Mr. P: "Snow on my *eye*lashes *(points to his eye)* . . ."

Children: *(point to their eyes)*

Mr. P: "I like best." Did you ever have a snowflake land on your eyelashes?

Children: Yeah!

Mr. P: What happened?

Sarah: It tickles.

Aidan: It melts.

Mr. P: It melted. How hot is your body?

Aidan: Like ninety-seven percent.

Mr. P: Ninety-eight degrees. So you melted that old snowflake. Well, let's see what else this girl likes. Are you ready to point in the right direction?

Children: Yeah!

Mr. P: Here's the next part. "*Grass* in the *east*, . . ."

Children: (*point*)

Mr. P: "*Grass* in the *west*, . . ."

Children: (*point*)

Mr. P: "Grass on my *knee* bones . . ."

Children: (*point to their knees*)

Mr. P: "I like best." How did she do that?

Children: Grass stains.

Mr. P: You think she's gonna get in trouble?

Children: Yeah!

Mr. P: I hope not. Here's another one. "*Light* in the *east*, . . ."

Children: (*point*)

Mr. P: "*Light* in the *west*, . . ."

Children: (*point*)

Mr. P: Where do you think she's gonna like—

Children: *Eyes!*

Mr. P: On her eyes? I like that idea.

Jennie: In her ears.

Mr. P: In her ears? (*laughs*)

Sam: On her hair.

Mr. P: "*Light* in my *win*dow . . ."

Children: Oh!

Mr. P: "I like best." See the lights in the window? (*shows the picture*)

Children: Yeah.

Mr. P: Here's the last part. "*Night* in the *east*, . . ."

Children: (*point*)

Mr. P: "*Night* in the *west*, . . ."

Children: (*point*)

Mr. P: Where do you think she might like it?

Children: Bed!

Mr. P: Let's see. "Night in my *own* . . ."

Children: Bed.

Mr. P: ". . . *bed* I like best." Ready to do it real fast?

Children: Yeah!

Mr. P: Can you point that quickly?

Children: Yeah!

Mr. P: Here we go. Got your fingers ready?

Mr. Porter goes on to read the poem again while the children point to the directions east and west and to their eyelashes and knees. On the last line, the children mimic going to bed. After the reading, Mr. Porter asks, "Who will help me read that one tomorrow?"

Mr. Porter hooks the children with the routine of pointing in the two directions and connecting to a song they had previously learned. After he expands the routine by pointing to his eyes, the children go on to point at appropriate times to parts of their bodies and the room. He helps the children make text-to-life connections, asking how experiences they have had are like those described in the poem. Finally, he asks them to predict the last words for the ending lines of the last two stanzas.

Note that Mr. Porter pauses for the children to fill in the final words of the stanza. This is known as an *oral cloze procedure*, and it is a key way that teachers involve children in read-alouds. Mr. Porter engages in an immediate rereading of the poem, with motions, and promises an additional reading the following day. Poems lend themselves naturally to repeated readings.

Mrs. Light's Poetry Discussion

Mr. Porter uses the word *part* to refer to a stanza of a poem. Mrs. Light, on the other hand, uses terms like *beat, line,* and *stanza* when discussing Eve Merriam's poem "You Be Saucer" with her second grade class. The poem is a 12-line lyric of three stanzas with two-beat lines, an *abcb* rhyme pattern, and a "You be *x* and I'll be *y*" sentence pattern. Unlike Mr. Porter's choreographed reading, this discussion is more open-ended, building on Mrs. Light's questions.

Mrs. Light: Do you like this poem (*points to the poem*)?

Children: Yeah!

Mrs. L: What is it that you like about it? Whitney?

Whitney: It rhymes good.

Mrs. L: Where does it rhyme?

Amy: *Night* and *tight.*

Max: *Good* and *night.*

Mrs. L: Do *good* and *night* rhyme?

Children: (*do not respond, but continue to raise their hands*)

Mrs. L: They kind of go together, but they don't rhyme. What else rhymes in this poem?

Philip: *Pears* and *stairs.*

Kelly: *Cup* and *up.*

Mrs. L: You notice anything interesting about the words that rhyme here? Tessa?

Tessa: They're all in the same place.

Mrs. L: What place are they?

Tessa: Um . . . first [*unclear*] cup [*unclear*]. Second [*unclear*] last [*unclear*].

Mrs. L: Okay. So the first rhyming word is at the end of the second line, always. And then where is the word that it rhymes with? Where is the next rhyming word?

Tessa: At the bottom of the last line.

Mrs. L: So you noticed that this poem has rhyme in it, okay? At the end of the second line and the end of the fourth line. What else do you notice? Derek?

Derek: You can imagine it.

Mrs. L: Tell me what you imagine.

Derek: Where it says, in the second stanza, I can imagine a pear tree with a whole bunch of pears on it. And on the first stanza, I can imagine a cup and saucer sitting on the table. And on the last one, I can imagine the mom tucking in the kid.

Mrs. L: Good. What else? Sadie?

Sadie: Like, *saucer* and *cup* go together. And pears are in a tree. And you say good night.

Mrs. L: Okay, so you've noticed in the first two lines that *saucer* and *cup* go together, and that *trees* and *pears* go together, and *good* and *night* go together (*points to the words on the poster*). That's great. What else? Edward?

Edward: I notice that you can find the title in the last stanza.

Mrs. L: Very good. (*reads*) "You be good, I'll be night." Excellent.

Edward: On the first stanza, it begins with "You be"; in the second it begins with "You be"; and in the third, it begins with "You be."

Mrs. L: Okay. You see another pattern. What else? Carrie?

Carrie: I noticed on the first sentence of each of 'em, like on the first one, it goes, "*piggy*back, *piggy*back." And on the second one it goes, "*carry* me, *carry* me." And on the third one it goes, "*tuck* me in, *tuck* me in." And they're all on the [*unclear*].

Mrs. L: Okay. So tell me what you see that is . . .

Carrie: I see that they repeat that two times, and on all the stanzas [*unclear*].

Mrs. L: Good. They're repeating the word or words on the third lines; they're repeating them twice. You noticed many things that I didn't notice, and I've read it many, many times. I started out by asking what you liked about the poem. Are you telling me that you like the pattern?

Children: Yeah.

Like many teachers, Mrs. Light begins discussions of poems by asking children for an aesthetic response—what they like about the poem—rather than asking what it means. Mrs. Light uses the children's responses to explore rhymes and where they occur in the poem. The teacher's open-ended questions allow children to have extended turns of talk and to bring up the images the poem evokes, words that go together semantically, the *you–I* sentence patterns, and the repeated phrase in the third line of each stanza. Mrs. Light notes the children's attention to language and emphasizes that even after many readings, there are still things to discover in poems. She concludes by linking the notion of language patterns with the pleasure that readers get from poems.

Both Mr. Porter and Mrs. Light give children opportunities to appreciate, participate in, and talk about highly patterned language. The children learn to participate verbally and nonverbally and to consider both the forms and the content of poems.

Children Explore the Question, "What Is a Poem?"

After K–2 children had read poems and prose stories with their teachers and on their own, we researchers asked them about differences between poems and stories. Their responses showed their developing understanding of the differences between poetry and prose. Daniel, a kindergartner, said, "A poem is a song and a story isn't. A poem is shorter. Poems are music. Poems you sing and stories you don't." Jessie, grade 1, said, "This [points to "Snow in the East"] is like a poem. But sometimes you can read it just without the poem. Just go like [reads slowly and with stress], 'Snow in the east.' But not with the little song that comes with it."

We asked children if all poems rhyme. Some agreed—"Yes, all of them do," said Matthew, grade 2—while others disagreed—"No, not all of them," said Jackie, grade 2. David, a first-grader, noticed repeated words at the beginning of lines: "This [points to "Snow in the East"] is a poem because it's got these words [points to the repeated line beginnings]. And that [points to the book *Rain Song*] is a story because it's got words in it. It doesn't repeat the same words like this [points to the lines in "Snow in the East"]."

Children agreed that poems are shorter in length than stories. Emily, grade 2, said, "[A poem's] not as long as a story would be, and [a story's] longer. There are more words on one page than like poems." Children pointed out that poems were written in shorter lines than prose, but they were uncertain about why this was so. Carter, grade 2, said, "Poems sometimes don't go all the way to the end. They stop in the middle." When we asked, "Why don't they write across the whole page?," Carter replied, "Because it would be a story." Jackie, grade 2, explained, "So they have more room for bigger pictures," while Emily, also grade 2, speculated, "Maybe they don't want you to think it's one long sentence. Maybe they are trying to make you think they are pages."

These answers show an emerging ability to speak about formal and functional differences between poetry and prose. The children who emphasized performance stated that poems are sung, not just read. The children who emphasized formal features highlighted rhyme, repeated words, shorter text overall, and shorter lines than prose.

By talking to children about poems and other texts, teachers can discover and promote children's developing understanding of language forms and functions. And by doing so, they also model and practice the vocabulary (*poem*, *prose*, *beat*, *rhyme*) used to talk about poems and other types of language.

Teaching Practices

The teachers who participated in our study routinely read poems more slowly and emphatically than prose, emphasizing formal features and pleasurable language. They read poems repeatedly and engaged children in performance, participation, and discus-

> We asked the children about differences between poems and stories. Their responses showed their developing understanding of the differences between poetry and prose.

Poems to Share With Young Children

Rhymes and Songs

A Collection of Favorite Rhymes, Songs and Concepts,
by David McPhail

The Fox Went Out on a Chilly Night: An Old Song
(Caldecott Honor Book), by Peter Spier

Frog Went A-Courtin' (Caldecott Medalist),
by John Langstaff, illus. by Feodor Rojankovsky

*Marc Brown's Playtime Rhymes: A Treasury for Families
to Learn and Play Together,* by Marc Brown

Over in the Meadow, by Ezra Jack Keats

The Silver Moon: Lullabies and Cradle Songs,
by Jack Prelutsky, illus. by Jui Ishida

There Was an Old Lady Who Swallowed a Fly,
by Simms Taback

This Old Man, by Carol Jones

Today Is Monday, by Eric Carle

To Market! To Market!, by Peter Spier

What a Wonderful World, by George David Weiss and
Bob Thiele, illus. by Ashley Bryan

You Be Good and I'll Be Night: Jump on the Bed Poems,
by Eve Merriam

Inventive Verse Picture Books

All By Myself!, by Aliki

All Kinds of Kids, by Christina Mia Gardeski,
illus. by Bob McMahon

Animals Born Alive and Well, by Ruth Heller

Casey at the Bat (Caldecott Honor Book),
by Ernest Lawrence Thayer, illus. by Christopher Bing

Compost Stew: An A to Z Recipe for the Earth,
by Mary McKenna Siddals, illus. by Ashley Wolff

Drummer Hoff (Caldecott Honor Book), adapted
by Barbara Emberley, illus. by Ed Emberley

Each Peach Pear Plum, by Janet and Allan Ahlberg

Hip Cat, by Jonathan London, illus. by Woodleigh
Hubbard

Love That Dog, by Sharon Creech

Many Luscious Lollipops: A Book About Adjectives,
by Ruth Heller

Owl Moon (Caldecott Medalist), by Jane Yolen,
illus. by John Schoenherr

A Sea Within a Sea: Secrets of the Sargasso,
by Ruth Heller

Shadow (Caldecott Medalist), trans. and illus.
by Marcia Brown

The Two of Them, by Aliki

sion and response. They included children's families and cultures. (For suggestions for other poems, see "Poems to Share With Young Children.")

Performance. Read poems slowly and with attention to the beat and the breaths that underlie the lines of poems. This lets children and teachers increase their awareness of and pleasure in language. Poems ask to be read repeatedly, and each rereading gives children insights into language, its uses, and its possible meanings.

Participation. As teachers read poems aloud and children pick up on the patterns within them, it seems natural for children to chime in. Children enjoy hearing favorites repeatedly and participating even more. Try using an oral cloze procedure—pause at a point where a language pattern permits children to predict what will come next (as demonstrated by Mr. Porter). This technique invites children to participate in reading along with an adult long before they read on their own. Encourage verbal and nonverbal participation. Read poems again and again to invite new, more complex ways for children to join in.

Discussion and response. Poems challenge and stretch a child's knowledge of word meanings and sentence patterns, and their knowledge of the sounds and syllables of spoken language and their connection to letters. Mrs. Light's open-ended "What Do You Notice?" technique invites children to share observations of all types. Teachers can expand and use these observations as teachable moments. Word study, word maps, and "Favorite Words" lists or posters are ways to focus on powerful words and their meanings.

Another strategy is to create a poem mix-up. Write a familiar poem on sentence strips. Cut it into sections, then mix them up and display them using a pocket chart. This gives children the opportunity to recognize and talk about patterns and for teachers to listen.

Family and cultural connections. Invite children and their families to share their oral culture: rhymes, songs, sayings, and proverbs. These can be written down, practiced, and discussed with children. Plan a family culture event where families are invited to recite favorite rhymes and poems as well as stories. This can be a great way to include children's cultures, especially when combined with food. In their discussions of poems, adult and child readers may imagine the situation or "world" implied by a poem, as Derek did in Mrs. Light's class. They may connect the world in the poem to the family and school worlds they inhabit and to other media they consume (books, TV shows, websites, and so on) (Elster 2000).

Conclusion

Age-appropriate poetry experiences promote young children's language awareness. Through repeated attention to language that is rich and personally meaningful, teachers and children study language while learning about the self and the world. Children build their understanding of written language, its parts, and its connection to spoken language from attention to sounds, syllables, words, and sentences.

Use poetry in the classroom to emphasize the meaningful experiences of poetry—group performance, interest in words and their meanings, discovery of the resources of language. To reduce poetry to a tool for learning about sounds would be a disservice to poetry and to children's learning needs. Our goal as teachers is to support children's awareness of the sounds, letters, and especially the meanings of words and their awareness of the importance of oral and written language for human collaboration.

> Through repeated attention to language that is rich and personally meaningful, teachers and children study language while learning about the self and the world.

References

Elster, C. 2000. "Entering and Opening the World of a Poem." *Language Arts* 78: 71–77.

Elster, C., & D. Hanauer. 2002. "Voicing Texts, Voices Around Texts: Reading Poems in Elementary School Classrooms." *Research in the Teaching of English* 37 (1): 89–134.

Faver, S. 2008. "Repeated Reading of Poetry Can Enhance Reading Fluency." *The Reading Teacher* 62 (4): 350–52.

Gill, S.R. 2007. "The Forgotten Genre of Children's Poetry." *The Reading Teacher* 60 (7): 622–25.

Holdaway, D. 1979. *The Foundations of Literacy.* Auckland: Ashton-Scholastic.

Kovalcik, B., & J.L. Certo. 2007. "The Poetry Café is Open! Teaching Literary Devices of Sound in Poetry Writing." *The Reading Teacher* 61 (1): 89–93.

McNair, J.C. 2012. "Poems About Sandwich Cookies, Jelly, and Chocolate: Poetry in K–3 Classrooms." *Young Children* 67 (4): 94–100.

NGACBP (National Governors Association Center for Best Practices) & CCSSO (Council of Chief State School Officers). 2010. *Common Core State Standards.* Washington, DC: NGACBP & CCSSO. www.corestandards.org/the-standards.

Rasinski, T., & B. Zimmerman. 2013. "What's the Perfect Text for Struggling Readers? Try Poetry!" *Reading Today* 30 (5): 15–16.

Yopp, H.K., & R.H. Yopp. 2009. "Phonological Awareness Is Child's Play!" *Young Children* 64 (1): 12–18, 21. www.naeyc.org/yc/pastissues/2009/january.

Debby Zambo

Young Girls Discovering Their Voice With Literacy and Readers Theater

Cindy teaches second grade in an urban school. She is concerned about the girls in the class, who are becoming somewhat cruel to their peers. Cliques of girls exclude other girls because they do not dress or act a certain way. To remedy this, Cindy needs to provide a way to help the girls find their inner voice—or true self—in a positive way. She decides these important goals can be accomplished with Readers Theater.

This opening scenario, drawn from visits to several classrooms, provides a glimpse into the beliefs and behaviors of young girls who have adopted an idealized notion of beauty. The ideal female, as portayed in the media, has a perfect body, owns many trendy and costly possessions, and is submissive and sexy. Young girls are easily influenced by the media's portrayal of teens and women, and therefore they may begin to form unrealistic ideas about beauty and begin to judge themselves and each other based on these unattainable standards (Brice Heath & Wolf 2005; Parke & Gauvain 2008). Teachers report hearing girls as young as 5 years old discussing their body flaws and planning to diet (Gurian 2010; Orenstein 2011). Cliques form, and some girls are excluded because they do not fit the image of the ideal female.

By the middle elementary grades, the self-esteem of many girls depends on particular ways of looking and acting, and more and more girls are unkind to peers who do not look or act a certain way (APA 2010). This way of thinking can lead to relational aggression, a covert form of bullying and ostracizing, among girls (Brizendine 2006; Kindlon 2006; Lamb & Brown 2006). Often, relational aggression has painful and long-lasting effects. Teachers are seeing girls engage in this type of aggression at an earlier age than ever before (Anthony & Lindert 2010).

Young girls may express relational aggression because they have lost their "voice" (Gilligan 1982; Gilligan et al. 2003). Voice is expressed *physically* with breath and sound, *psychologically* with emotions, and *culturally* with gendered ideals (Sperling & Appleman 2011). Having friends means everything to many young girls, so they may hide their true feelings, or lose their voice, to make or keep friends. Some girls spread rumors to avoid being ostracized, or they may try to buy friendship with their looks and possessions (Lamb & Brown 2006; Wohlwend 2009; Orenstein 2011).

Fortunately, it does not have to be this way—and literacy can help. Teachers can use book characters and important women in history to help girls hear strong female voices through activities like Readers Theater (Freeman 2007; Sprague & Keeting 2007). Readers Theater—cooperative dramatic reading from a text—gives children an opportunity to step into a strong character's shoes and hear and speak like that character. Reading and reflecting on narratives helps girls understand the challenges they face in making their own voices strong (Wolf 2008). As with other academic or social interventions, this literacy teaching strategy is most effective when implemented early in girls' development (Shonkoff & Phillips 2000; Stamm 2007). It is important to introduce girls to strong female voices as they begin to develop their voice, their self-concept, and their self-esteem.

Young girls need strong female role models because children as young as 4 may begin to think and act in socially stereotypical ways (Brizendine 2006). Children learn gender roles from models, and today girls find female models in the media. Girls observe role models and internalize the reinforcement they receive. For example, if a young girl sees a teenage actress wearing lip gloss and believes the actress has friends because of her beautiful lips, the young girl wants to wear lip gloss too. The young girl believes that wearing lip gloss will help her make friends. She may also reject other girls who do not wear lip gloss, because she believes they do not measure up to the ideal (Lamb & Brown 2006; Orenstein 2011).

On the other hand, if a young girl sees a happy, well-balanced female model behaving in nongendered ways, the girl will mimic her because she wants to experience the same positive reinforcement as the model (Wohlwend 2009). Thus, positive role models help girls find better ways to view themselves (Orenstein 2011).

Characters in books can become models for young children (Roberts & Crawford 2008). Book characters, just like Hollywood icons, show children either gendered or nongendered ways to act. The narratives in picture books can help young girls learn the stories of strong women and highlight their positive personal characteristics. After reading, girls can discuss their ideas and participate in activities that further expand their views. When children hear and discuss stories with others, they are more likely to openly express their ideas and feelings (Zambo 2010). As a result, children become more analytical and creative thinkers. Martinez, Roser, and Strecker (1999) find this to be especially true when children discover favorite characters to whom they become attached.

> When children hear and discuss stories with others, they are more likely to openly express their ideas and feelings.

Debby Zambo, PhD, is a member of the faculty of Mary Lou Fulton Teachers College at Arizona State University in Glendale. Before coming to the university, Debby taught young children with learning disabilities and emotional struggles. She now teaches undergraduate and graduate level educational psychology courses.

Websites With Scripts

Aaron Shepard's RT Page offers scripts for young readers in various genres (for example, folktales, fairy tales, tall tales, legends, myths, magical tales, fables, fantasy, humor, and historical fiction). It also has an online guide with information on staging, scripting, and performing. www.aaronshep.com/rt

Reader's Theatre Basics is a no-frills website with basic information on Readers Theater, ways to develop a script, student actor objectives, ready-made scripts, and books about Readers Theater. http://bms2.westport.k12.ct.us/mccormick/rt/RTHOME.htm

Research References for Reader's Theater provides sources for scripts, a downloadable teacher's guide, and a link to the Common Core State Standards addressed by Readers Theater. There is also a list of research showing that Readers Theater increases fluency, vocabulary, and comprehension. http://playbooks.com/readerstheaterresearch.shtml

Teaching Heart: Reader's Theater Scripts and Plays provides many scripts and other essentials, such as tips about voice inflection and the evaluation of performances. www.teachingheart.net/readerstheater.htm

Finding Heroines and Acting Out Roles

Using positive female characters as models for girls is a good starting point. However, library shelves full of books with excellent heroines do little unless those books are used in authentic ways—that is, ways that connect with the everyday lives of girls (Wohlwend 2009). Hearing a heroine's voice inside one's head while reading silently is very different from hearing that voice spoken out loud in a dramatic enactment. Openly voicing a character's words helps the reader learn the subtleties and nuances of how that character feels (Campbell & Cleland 2003).

Many teachers see this effect when young children engage in dramatic play. Dressing up, acting, and sounding like another person helps young children learn how others think, behave, and feel. Play is an important part of childhood and so is literacy (Connery, John-Steiner, & Marjanovic-Shane 2010). Girls need opportunities to voice strong words, and one way to accomplish this is through Readers Theater.

Readers Theater is similar to old-time radio plays in that it encourages an audience to conjure up images from the performers' words. The performers do not have to memorize their lines. They act with their voices, so typically there are no fancy costumes, staging, or props. Readers Theater allows children to gain a deeper understanding of the characters as they read their lines and act out their stories (Stewart 2008). Girls who speak the words of female protagonists learn what the characters are thinking and many times experience the emotions they feel.

Wohlwend (2009) contends that girls who play and act out alternative selves—imagining they are that person—challenge gender stereotypes. Alternate selves encourage imagination and creativity because they allow a child to become a character physically, mentally, and emotionally (Connery, John-Steiner, & Marjanovic-Shane 2010).

When girls perform during Readers Theater, they speak as strong female characters, feel the emotions the characters feel, tune in to their own true feelings, and find their voice (Campbell & Cleland 2003). Their performances allow for a new perspective on gender that has the potential to reduce the relational aggression seen in many classrooms (Kindlon 2006; Sprague & Keeling 2007). Teachers can use Readers Theater practice times and performances as opportunities to build communities of respect, responsibility, and interdependence.

Finding or Developing Scripts for Girls

Teachers frequently use Readers Theater to improve reading comprehension and fluency, enhance motivation, and build social skills. Martinez, Roser, and Strecker (1999) describe how use of Readers Theater with second-graders provided authentic opportunities for repeated readings and helped children improve their fluency and comprehension skills. Likewise, Campbell and Cleland (2003) find that Readers Theater allows teachers to cover academic standards, tap into children's multiple intelligences, and reduce anxiety in children who struggle with reading.

Researcher and teacher testimonials confirm the benefits of Readers Theater. However, using it in a gendered way to help young girls find the goodness inside themselves through role-playing strong female characters is a new and exciting concept. When girls understand themselves—or find their own voice—they realize they do not have to act in stereotypical ways or with relational aggression.

Teachers can adapt the approach to fit the needs and abilities of children in their classroom. Teachers who want to use Readers Theater with girls and boys can consult various sources to find appropriate scripts. For both girls and boys, scripts can focus on positive character traits like honesty, respect, tolerance, responsibility, perseverance, courage, and generosity (Zambo & Brozo 2009). Using Readers Theater to teach these traits helps teachers blend literacy and character education.

Many websites offer Readers Theater scripts and guidance (see "Websites With Scripts"). Teachers may also write their own scripts based on stories that their students enjoy.

When choosing stories for girls, look for a female protagonist with a strong voice whose story explains how she overcame challenges. Find stories that are substantive, lively, and at an appropriate reading level for the girls who will read them (Campbell & Cleland 2003). Familiar works with favorite characters are good starting points. The stories of beloved characters like Molly Lou Mellon, the fictional character in books by Patty Lovell, and Ruby Bridges, who was the first African American to integrate a New Orleans public school, are appropriate, interesting scripts for young girls (see "Books With Strong Female Characters," p. 86). Strive for balance when writing scripts from picture books. Make the script broad enough to capture the characters' voices and narrow enough to keep the readers focused and occupied.

Girls perform Readers Theater scripts with strong female protagonists, and boys do the same with scripts featuring male protagonists.

Enacting Scripts: Cindy's Use of Literacy and Readers Theater

The remainder of this article explains what happens as the 17 girls and 12 boys in Cindy's classroom prepare to present the scripts she developed in Readers Theater. Cindy assigns children to groups based on their gender. Girls perform Readers Theater scripts with strong female protagonists, and boys do the same with scripts featuring male protagonists.

As Cindy casts the characters for these scripts, she considers each child's personal, social, and emotional strengths and needs. For example, for some of the girls who act with relational aggression, Cindy might assign roles that address this behavior, such as

Books With Strong Female Characters

Abuela's Weave, by Omar S. Castañeda. Illus. by Enrique O. Sanchez. 1995. New York: Lee & Low Books. Abuela's livelihood is threatened because machine-made weavings are appearing in the markets, and because people are afraid of her birthmark. When she disguises her looks, Abuela saves the day, because curious onlookers purchase her weavings and other items.

Anna Banana and Me, by Lenore Blegvad. Illus. by Erik Blegvad. 1987. New York: Aladdin. Anna Banana is a fearless young girl who plays with a timid boy and eventually becomes his friend.

Beatrice's Goat, by Page McBrier. Illus. by Lori Lohstoeter. 2004. New York: Aladdin. Beatrice, a Ugandan girl, works hard to support her family, but her real dream is to go to school.

Boom Town, by Sonia Levitin. Illus. by Cat Bowman Smith. 1998. New York: Orchard. When her father seeks his fortune in gold out West, Amanda must move from the home she loves. Despite this hardship, Amanda becomes a hero. She forms her own business baking gooseberry pies, and her resources save the dying town.

Emma and the Silk Train, by Julie Lawson. Illus. by Paul Mombourquette. 1997. Toronto: Kids Can Press. Emma desperately wants some silk to make a dress. When a train derails, she works to achieve this goal by gathering the silk that has spilled out.

Fire Station Number 4: The Daily Life of Firefighters, by Mary T. Fortney. Photos by Norbert von der Groeben. 1999. Minneapolis: Carolrhoda Books. The story depicts a typical day of three Livermore, California, firefighters. The book provides unique information on apparatus, women firefighters, and fire safety and prevention.

High as a Hawk: A Brave Girl's Historic Climb, by T.A. Barron. Illus. by Ted Lewin. 2004. New York: Philomel. This is the true story of 8-year-old Harriet Peters, the youngest person to climb Long's Peak.

Little Granny Quarterback, by Bill Martin Jr. and Michael Sampson. Illus. by Michael Chesworth. 2001. Honesdale, PA: Boyds Mills Press. Spunky Granny, who was a star quarterback in her day, leaps into her television to help her favorite team.

Mailing May, by Michael O. Tunnell. Illus. by Ted Rand. 1997. New York: HarperCollins. Because May is unable to afford a train ticket to visit her grandmother, her Uncle Leonard mails her on a delightful journey.

Mama and Me and the Model T, by Faye Gibbons. Illus. by Ted Rand. 1999. New York: Morrow Junior Books/HarperCollins. When the new Model T arrives, Mama proves to her family that she can drive just as fast and courageously as any man.

Mary Smith, by Andrea U'Ren. 2003. New York: Farrar, Straus, & Giroux. Mary Smith has a very untraditional job as a waker-upper. She blows peas at doors to wake up people for work.

My Mother Is a Doctor, by Charnan Simon. Illus. by Patrick Girouard. 2006. New York: Child's World. This is a child's story of living with a mother who has a fast-paced, life-saving career.

The Name Jar, by Yangsook Choi. 2003. New York: Dragonfly Books. Unhei moves to the United States from Korea and is embarrassed by her unpronounceable name.

Officer Brown Keeps Neighborhoods Safe, by Alice K. Flanagan. 1999. New York: Children's Press. The book takes you through the day of Officer Deborah Hawes-Brown, deputy chief of the Hartford, Connecticut, Police Department, as she works to keep children safe.

The Other Side, by Jacqueline Woodson. Illus. by E.B. Lewis. 2001. New York: Putnam Juvenile. Two racially different girls cross a symbolic fence despite warnings from their mothers.

Something Beautiful, by Sharon Dennis Wyeth. Illus. by Chris K. Soentpiet. 2002. New York: Dragonfly Books. A girl who lives in poverty takes on the challenge to find beauty in her world.

Stand Tall, Molly Lou Melon, by Patty Lovell. Illus. by David Catrow. 2001. New York: Penguin Putnam. Molly Lou Melon must move away from the grandmother who loves her and attend a new school. Being small and funny looking, Molly Lou becomes the subject of bullying until she turns the tide.

The Story of Ruby Bridges, by Robert Coles. Illus. by George Ford. 2010. New York: Scholastic Paperback. This is the story of a courageous girl, Ruby Bridges, who attended a New Orleans elementary school after court-ordered desegregation in 1960.

a character who is bullied. This helps them understand how it feels to be bullied. Cindy also ensures that each character has lines of equal importance and length so children will not feel embarrassed when reading their parts. To engage children who struggle with reading and to provide inconspicuous support, she makes sure their lines contain high-interest content, repeated phrases, and familiar vocabulary. Cindy assigns their parts, previews difficult vocabulary, and provides mini-lessons in decoding strategies. The assignment for all of the children includes reading their parts to peers and to family members at home.

Building literacy skills is important, but Cindy is more interested in the transformative power of literacy. Voice is expressed *physically* with breath and sound and *psychologically* with emotions, so for some scripts, Cindy makes sure girls who display relational aggression—that is, the girls with lost voices—find their voice by reading the words of strong female protagonists.

The task is not easy for some girls. For example, Mara—whose self-esteem appears to be based on how she looks and what clothes and toys she possesses—struggles to say the words of the main character in Andrea U'Ren's book, *Mary Smith*. Mary was a bold and brave woman who had an unusual job as a "waker-upper." Armed with a peashooter and other noisy objects, Mary Smith acted as a human alarm clock who woke the town's workers with noise. Cindy helps Mara by modeling Mary Smith's bold and forceful voice. Mara practices raising and lowering the volume, pitch, and tone of her voice; altering the pace of her delivery; varying stress on words and syllables; and projecting her voice into an open room.

Cindy also leads Mara and the other girls in warm-up activities. They imagine they are characters like Astute Annie, Brave Barbara, and Eager Esther (these are characters you may create in your classroom). During the warm-ups, the girls face each other and think up short lines to voice. For example, Brave Barbara may say she is not afraid of the dark, and Eager Esther may say that she is always ready to accept a challenge, like standing up for someone who is being bullied. These warm-up sessions get the girls ready to take on their larger roles.

For other Readers Theater productions, Cindy assigns major roles to girls excluded from cliques. She assigns smaller Readers Theater parts to girls with lost voices, the girls who have bullied or ostracized others. The girls who do not receive major roles become angry and emotional. Cindy acknowledges their hurt feelings and, in a side conversation, tells them that each part, big or small, contributes to the overall production.

Cindy helps everyone understand that all contributions matter and that each person has a responsibility and value to the production team.

Cindy expects the girls to respect each other and the roles they have been assigned as they work on Readers Theater. She invites each girl to use her voice to the best of her ability, and says each girl has the right to be heard. If a girl makes a mistake, Cindy offers ideas to help her step into her character's shoes, feel her emotions, and find her voice. If a girl becomes critical or makes fun of others and their mistakes, Cindy takes her aside. She reviews what she has been seeing, and asks the girl to explain what she is doing and why. The girl and Cindy then problem solve appropriate behaviors and words. Cindy helps the girls see that struggles with parts and errors in reading are opportunities to learn and grow.

Cindy expects the girls to interact as a community of learners and to accept responsibility for their production. The girls negotiate daily goals with Cindy, and she monitors their commitments as they work on Readers Theater scripts. Over the first week, Cindy sees improvements in the girls' sense of responsibility and in the community atmosphere.

Marti, a popular girl assigned a small role, announces that she will work with Alora, a less popular girl who has the leading part in Omar Castañeda's *Abuela's Weave*. Cindy realizes this is not easy for Marti, because she wants the lead, so she closely monitors the girls. Cindy points out to Marti the importance of her part and how this part is key to the overall production. Cindy also helps Marti understand that even with a small part, she can help others like Alora. Marti can listen to Alora read her lines and make sure the correct words are read.

From the discussion Marti sees the importance of her small part and gains insight into how she can contribute to the learning of her peers. This helps Marti and Alora see themselves as equals. As the girls in the class begin to help each other and work together, Cindy notices a decrease in incidences of name-calling, spreading rumors, and excluding peers from activities.

Cindy encourages interdependence, such as that shown by Marti and Alora, as she begins removing the scaffolding she has offered children whose reading skills are at a lower level than that of others in the class. When children pose questions, Cindy refrains from immediately supplying answers. She asks the girls, "What do you think?" and helps them negotiate resolutions. Cindy builds interdependence by giving pairs or triads of girls small, manageable challenges to complete together. For example, Cindy might ask the girls to help their partner say her lines with expression or select important words from one of the parts and perform them with both body and voice. Another challenge might be closing their eyes, envisioning their partner successfully reading her role, and then telling her about the experience.

The classroom focus on respect, responsibility, and interdependence leads to wonderful performances and celebrations. When Melissa, who tends to keep to herself, confidently voices the words of the self-sufficient Amanda in a performance of Sonia Levitin's *Boom Town*, the girls give her a standing ovation. When Alora, a dual language learner who is often reluctant to speak up, voices Abuela's words, the girls rush to give her a hug. When Marti and the other girls who were cruel play their small parts, everyone cheers.

As the girls in the class begin to help each other and work together, Cindy notices a decrease in incidences of name-calling, spreading rumors, and excluding peers.

The boys, who are also a part of the classroom community, act respectfully, sitting on the edge of their seats as Julie Lawson's Emma gets swept away by the current. They cheer when Andrea U'Ren's Mary Smith shoots her peas. During Readers Theater performances, all ears listen to the girls' voices and all eyes witness their confidence. The girls find their voice as they absorb and speak the words of strong female protagonists for themselves and their peers.

Moving Forward

Although Readers Theater has already led to a decrease in relational aggression, Cindy knows she must continue preventing and addressing the problem. Participation in Readers Theater helps the girls learn from female protagonists, but it is also important to learn from real women. In the weeks to come, both girls and boys work on several activities. The suggestions described below include specifics related to building girls' voices, but educators can also adapt them for the boys in their class.

Community models. Invite women working in nontraditional jobs (such as a highway construction worker, police officer, or firefighter) to visit the class to discuss their jobs. Before the visits, introduce relevant children's books (for example, Alice Flanagan's *Officer Brown Keeps Neighborhoods Safe*, Charnan Simon's *My Mother Is a Doctor*, and M.T. Fortney's *Fire Station Number 4: The Daily Life of Firefighters*). Have the girls perform Readers Theater scripts based on the women featured in the books.

Adult females as teachers. Ask female family members to visit the class to share a talent such as carpentry, cooking, or painting. Choose books related to the talents shared that children can read and discuss.

Sport sisters. Invite female athletes from local middle and high schools to visit the class. They can talk with the girls about their sports and, when possible, demonstrate skills. Children can read and discuss books related to the sports and practice the skills at recess.

Female buddies. Have adolescent girls from civic or neighborhood groups like the Girl Scouts serve as buddies for the younger children. Each pair of buddies can work on reading, writing, math, art, music, and other subjects.

House construction and truck driving. Set up centers with games and activities that boys are typically drawn to, such as materials to paint and build with and noisy objects to create sounds. Encourage girls to explore materials they may never have tried before.

These activities and others can stretch girls to try new things and play with new objects. They can also expand young girls' horizons and let them hear strong voices and see female characters in nontraditional roles. Activities like these, along with Readers Theater, create an environment where girls can be themselves, expand their views of gender, and find a voice of their own. Girls can gain insight from and become transformed by the texts they read, the voices they hear, and the activities they do.

References

Anthony, M., & R. Lindert. 2010. *Little Girls Can Be Mean: Four Steps to Bully-Proof Girls in the Early Grades*. New York: St. Martin's Griffin.

APA (American Psychological Association). 2010. "Report of the APA Task Force on the Sexualization of Girls." Washington, DC: APA. www.apa.org/pi/women/programs/girls/report-full.pdf.

Brice Heath, S., & S.A. Wolf. 2005. *Dramatic Learning in the Primary School*. London: Creative Partnerships.

Brizendine, L. 2006. *The Female Brain*. New York: Broadway Books.

Campbell, M., & J.V. Cleland. 2003. *Readers Theatre in the Classroom: A Manual for Teachers of Children and Adults*. Bloomington, IN: IUniverse.

Connery, M.C., V.P. John-Steiner, & A. Marjanovic-Shane, eds. 2010. *Vygotsky and Creativity: A Cultural-Historical Approach to Play, Meaning Making, and the Arts*. New York: Peter Lang.

Freeman. J. 2007. *Once Upon a Time: Using Storytelling, Creative Drama, and Reader's Theater with Children in Grades PreK–6*. Westport, CT: Greenwood Publishing Group.

Gilligan, C. 1982. *In a Different Voice: Psychological Theory and Women's Development*. Cambridge, MA: Harvard University Press.

Gilligan, C., R. Spencer, M.K. Weinberg, & T. Bertsch. 2003. "On the Listening Guide: A Voice-Centered Relational Method." In *Qualitative Research in Psychology: Expanding Perspectives in Methodology and Design*, eds. P.M. Camic, J.E. Rhodes, & L. Yardley. 157–72. Washington, DC: American Psychological Association.

Gurian, M. 2010. *Boys and Girls Learn Differently! A Guide for Teachers and Parents*. 10th ed. San Francisco: Jossey-Bass.

Kindlon, D. 2006. *Alpha Girls: Understanding the New American Girl and How She Is Changing the World*. New York: Rodale.

Lamb, S., & L.M. Brown. 2006. *Packaging Girlhood: Rescuing Our Daughters from Marketers' Schemes*. New York: St. Martin's Griffin.

Martinez, M., N.L. Roser, & S. Strecker. 1999. "'I Never Thought I Could Be a Star': A Reader's Theatre Ticket to Fluency." *The Reading Teacher* 52 (4): 326–34.

Orenstein. P. 2011. *Cinderella Ate My Daughter: Dispatches From the Front Lines of the New Girlie-Girl Culture*. New York: HarperCollins.

Parke, R.D. & M. Gauvain. 2008. *Child Psychology: A Contemporary Viewpoint*. 7th ed. Boston: McGraw Hill.

Roberts, S.K., & P.A. Crawford. 2008. "Real-Life Calls for Real Books: Literature to Help Children Cope With Family Stressors." *Young Children* 63 (5): 12–17. www.naeyc.org/files/yc/file/200809/Crawford.pdf.

Shonkoff, J.P., & D.A. Phillips, eds. 2000. *From Neurons to Neighborhoods: The Science of Early Childhood Development*. Washington, DC: National Academies Press.

Sprague, M.M., & K.K. Keeling. 2007. *Discovering Their Voices: Engaging Adolescent Girls With Young Adult Literature*. Newark, DE: International Reading Association.

Sperling, M., & D. Appleman. 2011. "Voice in the Context of Literacy Studies." *Reading Research Quarterly* 46 (1): 70–84.

Stamm, J. 2007. *Bright From the Start: The Simple Science-Backed Way to Nurture Your Child's Developing Mind, From Birth to Age 3*. New York: Gotham Books.

Stewart, M. 2008. "The Science of Readers Theater." *Reading Today* 26 (3): 44.

Wohlwend, K.E. 2009. "Damsels in Discourse: Girls Consuming and Producing Identity Texts Through Disney Princess Play." *Reading Research Quarterly* 44 (1): 57–83.

Wolf, M. 2008. *Proust and the Squid: The Story and Science of the Reading Brain*. New York: HarperCollins.

Zambo, D., & W.G. Brozo. 2009. *Bright Beginnings for Boys: Engaging Young Boys in Active Literacy*. Newark, DE: The International Reading Association.

Zambo, D. 2010. "Using Picture Books and Literary Experiences to Help Boys and Girls Develop Literacy and Socio-Emotional Skills." In *Perspectives on Gender in Early Childhood*, ed. T. Jacobson, 127–54. St. Paul, MN: Redleaf.

María Paula
Ghiso

Every Language Is Special:
Promoting Dual Language Learning in Multicultural Primary Schools

The changing demographics of neighborhoods and schools require that all educators consider how to support children who are developing bilingualism and biliteracy (Cummins et al. 2005). Research documents the importance of engaging young children in learning by drawing on community heritages and cultural and linguistic resources, and of connecting more effectively with families (Campano 2007; Genishi & Dyson 2009). Such inclusive pedagogies are especially important in light of two contradictory trends: increasingly diverse school populations, with children and families from varied backgrounds and with a range of immigration and other life experi-

ences, and the erosion of dual language and bilingual programs in some communities and school systems. Given the impact of children's home resources on their academic, social, and identity development, educators must think of creative ways to provide multilingual school experiences.

In this article, I invite readers to a school district with children from approximately 69 countries (the top 10 represented are Bangladesh, Liberia, India, Pakistan, Vietnam, Jamaica, Ecuador, Sierra Leone, China, and Haiti) who speak 89 different home languages, including Spanish, Bengali, Vietnamese, Punjabi, Chinese, Urdu, Arabic, and French. The district does not

we went to chucke chees and we invited chucke
My aunt took a picture of me hi filling chuke and we ate
cake and pizza. We play lots of games. When we finished
playing we got little tickets to buy toys In yellow shirt is me
in purple shirt is my bro and chads e in black shirt
is my dad in light green shirt is my mom and in dark
green shirt is my aunt and my little cosin. And in orange
shirt is my aunts mother.

María Paula Ghiso, EdD, is assistant professor in the Department of Curriculum and Teaching at Teachers College, Columbia University. Her research and teaching focus on literacy learning in early childhood and multilingual contexts.

Children's work samples courtesy of the author.

Author's Note: I would like to thank Mrs. Rangan for welcoming me into her classroom, and her school district for supporting such inclusive practices.

have bilingual programs, but educators have advocated for dual language learning through other means. In the sections that follow, I focus on an elementary school summer program for emergent bilinguals (García & Kleifgen 2010) led by Mrs. Rangan, a district English language learning teacher, as an example of inclusive practices that reimagine the relationship between home and school.

Tapping the Cultural Resources of Educators

Research often focuses on the differences between mainstream educators and the diversity of children and families. However, educators themselves are cultural beings with varied languages (including multiple English dialects), and their backgrounds may be useful in promoting multicultural learning and global sensitivity in early childhood classrooms. I was lucky to experience this firsthand through my research collaboration with Mrs. Rangan.

During the summer program, Mrs. Rangan had a class of 7- and 8-year-old children who were in various phases of learning English, from those who had recently arrived in the United States and spoke only a few words of English to children with more intermediate and advanced proficiency. Mrs. Rangan and I looked for ways to support the children's English acquisition, but not at the expense of their home languages and cultural heritages. Our backgrounds as immigrants from India and Argentina, respectively, were important resources for understanding the tensions some children may have been experiencing, and for supporting them in explorations of their own (and each other's) languages and literacies.

One important consideration was the pressure for children to value English over their own languages and cultures exerted in politics and in the media, especially when the academic curriculum focused on English only. Mrs. Rangan continually discussed with the children the importance of each of their backgrounds as a source of knowledge and encouraged mutual learning. Morning meetings and shared reading became times for supporting cross-cultural understanding. For example, each day during circle time one child taught the class a greeting in his home language, which the children and teachers then used to welcome one another. Although Mrs. Rangan herself is multilingual, she did not know all the children's languages and looked to them to serve as her teachers.

Mrs. Rangan exemplified this attitude one morning in a daily message written on chart paper to the children. The letter began, "Dear Knowledgeable Knights," and went on to recount the date, the weather, and a special event planned for that day. The children read the message together, commented on its content, identified punctuation and specific word sounds, and discussed vocabulary. Mrs. Rangan focused on the word *knowledgeable,* using it to refer to the children's and families' many resources and to position herself as learning from them. She noted,

> Because you are so knowledgeable, I want you to teach me something about your family and your culture. In my house, I always make my traditional chicken curry, which my mother used to make and my grandmother used to make. Even though we are in America, we still have things from our countries. We have many teachers that come from different places. We have so many students from different countries. Guess what? Here you can be yourself.

Mrs. Rangan referred to the children as knights because, as she emphasized, like the heroes in fairy tales, they are fighting for good—for an education, for opportunities, and for justice—even in the face of obstacles or unfamiliar situations.

There is much to learn from Mrs. Rangan's words. She explicitly told the children that they come with knowledge, countering the misconceptions that immigrant children arrive at school lacking experiences and as blank slates. Mrs. Rangan also aligned teachers and children—noting that both groups possess diverse traditions and legacies and must navigate their identities within the culture of school. By referring to the children as knights who "fight for opportunity and justice," Mrs. Rangan acknowledged that "being yourself" and maintaining your culture and language is political, and that children must advocate for themselves and their families.

Throughout the summer program, Mrs. Rangan intertwined her teaching with comments that conveyed to the children the value of their experiences:

> We have different situations, but one thing is clear—we all have roots. It is so important for us to be proud of our home country and our home language. Just remember one thing—no country or language is any less important than English. Every language is special.

The frequent use of *we* underscored the shared experiences between Mrs. Rangan and the children. As a teacher who understood the difficulties of navigating a new culture and assimilationist messages in school, Mrs. Rangan elevated the status of children's home languages and fostered cross-cultural understanding, despite policies and messages that tend to value English.

Learning From Community Literacies

Mrs. Rangan and I sought to create school settings inclusive of the children's knowledge and experiences. We infused the curriculum with multicultural and bilingual children's literature, invited children to tell family stories, encouraged them to include their home languages in their writing, and shared our own immigration histories.

ありがとう いつも しごと
をがんばってくれて！
きらは おかあさんの日

Dear mom
Thank you for the
working hard!
Today is
Mothers
day.

The children's diversity presented a variety of scenarios. Some children could read and write in their home languages but did not yet speak English; others were orally fluent in their home languages but were unfamiliar with those writing systems; and for some children—those who had arrived in the United States at a very young age or had been born here—the dichotomies of terms like *home language* and *new language* did not apply. How, then, could we two educators support multilingual literacies, especially when we knew only some of the children's languages? We found promise in looking beyond the classroom to family and community resources.

Families as Partners

Parents became invaluable partners to Mrs. Rangan and her class. The district sponsored an adult English as a second language program alongside the one for the children, intentionally housing it at the same location to facilitate child care and capitalize on family presence at the school. Mrs. Rangan encouraged the children's families to join her class when they were not in the adult courses. Mrs. Arain, Salim's mother, became a regular fixture throughout the summer—participating in circle time activities, helping teachers, sharing artifacts from her own culture, and growing increasingly more comfortable in the classroom despite her emergent proficiency in English.

When one of the Pakistani children wanted to include Urdu text in a story he was writing in English, Mrs. Arain stepped in. They collaborated to translate his work, with the child focusing on the English and Mrs. Arain on the Urdu writing. The text in English illustrates the blended influences that make up children's lives: the topic and setting—a birthday party at Chuck E. Cheese's—describe a popular American scenario, while the careful enumeration of extended family and the bilingual writing depict the culturally inflected nature of the experience. The piece underscores how young children's realities encompass multiple worlds. (See p. 92.)

Mrs. Rangan viewed Salim's mother as possessing essential funds of knowledge (Moll & González 2004) for nurturing students' dual languages. This contrasts with the viewpoint held by some that immigrant families lack useful skills and knowledge.

Writing in Other Languages

In encouraging writing in multiple languages, we asked the children to turn to others in their home or school community who, like Mrs. Arain, had expertise in these areas. Mrs. Rangan and I contributed the languages we knew, and we supported the children as they looked for other partners (relatives, community members, and older children), used resources such as translation dictionaries or technologies, and wrote as best they could without overemphasis on grammatical conventions.

Kalu, a 7-year-old from Nigeria, for example, was composing a story about a trip to the water park. (See p. 93.) He wanted to include writing in one of his home languages, Yoruba, but he did not know how. I suggested that he select one word that encapsulated the essence of his story and try to sound it out. Kalu combined his literacy in English and his oral fluency in Yoruba to write down an approximation of the word *play* (*ÿiré*)—*ari*—which he framed at the bottom of his page below the English text. I encouraged him to continue writing in Yoruba and connected him with a fourth grader in the summer program who was also from Nigeria.

Jin had a different trajectory. Born and raised in Japan and of Japanese and Liberian descent, Jin arrived in the district at the end of second grade. Mrs. Rangan was one of the teachers assigned to work with her. In class, Mrs. Rangan and her teaching partner invited the children to write Mother's Day cards to a family member. Upon reflection, they realized that this activity could exclude some children and families. Newcomers like Jin would not be able to fully express themselves in English, and immigrant families might not understand the English messages meant for them. The teachers redesigned the lesson by asking children to compose a message in their home languages and in English. (See p. 94.) In doing this, they kept the literacy intent of the activity and also conveyed the importance of multilingual communication within diverse environments.

Creating Networks Between Home and School

Research identifies how language and culture may be seen as barriers to parent participation in their children's schooling (Souto-Manning 2010). In a diverse setting, educators are unlikely to know all the languages spoken by children and families. However, when educators take an inquiry stance (Cochran-Smith & Lytle 2009) into their practice—where they investigate dissonances, learn from their

Ways to Support Dual Language Learning and Home–School Connections

- Learn about the languages and literacies of the children and families in your school. What languages are spoken in their countries? What languages are privileged over others? What are characteristics of the writing practices? Learn by asking dual language parents and community organizations, looking in print resources and online, or making this a collaborative inquiry with your class.

- Investigate the resources available in your school, district, and community. What translation services are available? What information do various individuals (social workers, dual language learner teachers, classroom teachers, family members, community organizations) have? How can you share this information? Find dual language support in your area—whether at school, in the area, or online.

- Read picture books that include languages other than English, even if you are unfamiliar with the language. If you are not sure how to pronounce a word, ask a child in your class or a family member. Invite a child or parent to read a story in their language or tell a story through pictures.

- Invite children to teach the class a word in their home language. Take turns using these words in the classroom. Emphasize that everyone has important knowledge and can learn from one another.

- Encourage children to use all the languages they know. Discuss learning multiple languages with the children. When do children use each language and why? What languages do their family members speak? What are the benefits of knowing more than one language? Create literacy opportunities for children to convey stories using visuals and words in all the languages they know.

- Invite families into the school. Ask for volunteers to share a family story (in English or their home language), a photograph, or a cultural practice, or to help out in the classroom. Host a get-together before school, after school, or in the evening for families of the same language group and have a translator present. If an interpreter is unavailable through your district, invite a bilingual parent, community member, or high school student to take on this role. Be open to learning from families' insights.

students, and question the sociopolitical nature of schooling—what appears to be a barrier might instead be a unique opportunity for collaboration.

Mrs. Rangan successfully tapped district resources to help her advocate for students and cultivate relationships with families. As one of the Spanish translators working with Mrs. Rangan, I gained a deep appreciation for the networks she created through her deliberate and time-intensive orchestration. She facilitated home–school interactions through use of district interpreters, who she consistently paired with the same families in order to build relationships. As Mrs. Rangan noted, a particular Bengali translator played an important role in making several families feel welcome and comfortable in the school.

These efforts made it possible for families to seek support for children's health care, ask questions about educational practices, and express personal struggles—which led educators to plan home-language get-togethers where families could connect. Mrs. Rangan and the network of translators also facilitated families' opportunities to share their insights and knowledge with school personnel. Mrs. Rangan's own experiences influenced this approach. As a newcomer to the country, she had been encouraged to volunteer in her daughter's class, and this led her to pursue teaching certification and become a teacher.

Conclusion

The teaching practices of Mrs. Rangan and her colleagues reflect a language-as-resource orientation (Ruiz 1984) in teaching children from diverse backgrounds and connecting with their families. They recognize families as partners in dual language education and immigrant students as cosmopolitan intellectuals (Campano & Ghiso 2011) whose experiences can lead the school community in cultivating global sensibilities. The efforts highlighted in this article show how educators and families can work together to encourage linguistic and cultural diversity.

References

Campano, G. 2007. *Immigrant Students and Literacy: Reading, Writing, and Remembering.* New York: Teachers College Press.

Campano, G., & M.P. Ghiso. 2011. "Immigrant Students as Cosmopolitan Intellectuals." Chap. 12 in *Handbook of Research on Children's and Young Adult Literature*, eds. S.A. Wolf, K. Coats, P. Enciso, & C.A. Jenkins, 164–76. New York: Routledge.

Cochran-Smith, S., & S.L. Lytle. 2009. *Inquiry as Stance: Practitioner Research in the Next Generation.* New York: Teachers College Press.

Cummins, J., V. Bismilla, P. Chow, S. Cohen, F. Giampapa, L. Leoni, P. Sandhu, & P. Sastri. 2005. "Affirming Identity in Multilingual Classrooms." *Educational Leadership* 63 (1): 38–43. www.ascd.org/ASCD/pdf/journals/ed_lead/el200509_cummins.pdf.

García, O. & J. Kleifgen. 2010. *Educating Emergent Bilinguals: Policies, Programs, and Practices for English Language Learners.* New York: Teachers College Press.

Genishi, C., & A.H. Dyson. 2009. *Children, Language, and Literacy: Diverse Learners in Diverse Times.* New York: Teachers College Press.

Moll, L.C., & N. González. 2004. "Engaging Life: A Funds-of-Knowledge Approach to Multicultural Education." Chap. 33 in *Handbook of Research on Multicultural Education*, 2nd ed., eds. J.A. Banks & C.A.M. Banks, 669–715. San Francisco: Jossey-Bass.

Ruiz, R. 1984. "Orientations in Language Planning." NABE: *The Journal of the National Association for Bilingual Education* 8 (2): 15–34.

Souto-Manning, M. 2010. "Family Involvement: Challenges to Consider, Strengths to Build On." *Young Children* 65 (2): 82–88.

Resources for Supporting Young Children's Language and Literacy

NAEYC Resources

Ableser, J. 2008. "Authentic Literacy Experiences to Teach and Support Young Children During Stressful Times." *Young Children* 63 (2): 74–79.

Baker, I., & M. Baker Schiffer. 2005–2014. The Reading Chair. *Young Children* column. www.naeyc.org/yc/columns/readingchair.

Barrett-Mynes, J., M.J. Moran, & D. Tegano. 2010. "Supporting Struggling Readers: Using Interactive Read-Alouds and Graphic Organizers." *Voices of Practitioners* 5 (2): 1–12.

Baskwill, J., & M.J. Harkins. 2009. "Children, Parents, and Writing: Using Photography in a Family Literacy Workshop." *Young Children* 64 (5) 28–33.

Bates, C.C. 2013. "Flexible Grouping During Literacy Centers: A Model for Differentiating Instruction." *Young Children* 68 (2): 30–33.

Birckmayer, J., A. Kennedy, & A. Stonehouse. 2008. *From Lullabies to Literature: Stories in the Lives of Infants and Toddlers*. Washington, DC: NAEYC.

Brereton, A.E. 2010. "Is Teaching Sign Language in Early Childhood Classrooms Feasible for Busy Teachers and Beneficial for Children?" *Young Children* 65 (4): 92–97.

Brinson, S.A. 2007. "Boys Booked on Barbershops: A Cutting-Edge Literacy Program." *Young Children* 62 (2): 42–48.

Brown, K.M. 2010. "Young Authors: Writing Workshop in Kindergarten." *Young Children* 65 (1): 24–28.

Cheatham, G.A., & Y.E. Ro. 2010. "Young English Learners' Interlanguage as a Context for Language and Early Literacy Development." *Young Children* 65 (4): 18–23.

Chen, J.J., & S.H. Shire. 2011. "Strategic Teaching: Fostering Communication Skills in Diverse Young Learners." *Young Children* 66 (2): 20–27.

Christ, T., & X.C. Wang. 2012. "Supporting Preschoolers' Vocabulary Learning: Using a Decision-Making Model to Select Appropriate Words and Methods." *Young Children* 67 (2): 74–80. www.naeyc.org/yc/files/yc/file/201203/Christ_YC0311.pdf.

Copple, C., & S. Bredekamp, eds. 2009. *Developmentally Appropriate Practice in Early Childhood Programs Serving Children From Birth Through Age 8*. 3rd ed. Washington, DC: NAEYC.

Correia, M.P. 2011. "Fiction vs. Informational Texts: Which Will Kindergartners Choose?" *Young Children* 66 (6): 100–104. www.naeyc.org/yc/files/yc/file/201111/Correia_Fiction_vs_Informational_Texts_Online%201111.pdf.

DeBey, M., & D. Bombard. 2007. "Expanding Children's Boundaries: An Approach to Second-Language Learning and Cultural Understanding." *Young Children* 62 (2): 88–93.

DeBruin-Parecki, A. 2008. *Effective Early Literacy Practice: Here's How, Here's Why*. Baltimore: Brookes.

Special thanks to Sue Mankiw and Karen N. Nemeth for their contributions to this resource list. Sue is an assistant professor and director of the early childhood teaching program at William Paterson University. Karen is an author, presenter, consultant, and founder of Language Castle, a website offering resources for teachers of dual language learners.

Duke, N.K. 2003. "Reading to Learn From the Very Beginning: Information Books in Early Childhood." *Young Children* 58 (2): 14–20.

Exley, B., J. Burton, & J. Barnett. 2007. "Australian Children Catch the Bug: Motivating Young Children to Engage in Reading." *Young Children* 62 (6): 36–40.

Gaffney, J.S., M.M. Ostrosky, & M.L. Hemmeter. 2008. "Books as Natural Support for Young Children's Literacy Learning." *Young Children* 63 (4): 87–93.

Genishi, C., & A.H. Dyson. 2009. *Children, Language, and Literacy: Diverse Learners in Diverse Times*. New York: Teachers College Press; Washington, DC: NAEYC.

Hammack, B.G., M.M. Foote, S. Garretson, & J. Thompson. 2012. "Family Literacy Packs: Engaging Teachers, Families, and Young Children in Quality Activities to Promote Partnerships for Learning." *Young Children* 67 (3): 104–10.

Jalongo, M.R. 2004. *Young Children and Picture Books*. 2nd ed. Washington, DC: NAEYC.

Jalongo, M.R. 2008. *Learning to Listen, Listening to Learn: Building Essential Skills in Young Children*. Washington, DC: NAEYC.

Johnson, M.H. 2008. "Developing Verbal and Visual Literacy Through Experiences in the Visual Arts: 25 Tips for Teachers." *Young Children* 63 (1): 74–79.

Kalmar, K. 2008. "Let's Give Children Something to Talk About: Oral Language and Preschool Literacy." *Young Children* 63 (1): 88–92.

Kara-Soteriou, J., & H. Rose. 2008. "A Bat, a Snake, a Cockroach, and a Fuzzhead: Using Children's Literature to Teach About Positive Character Traits." *Young Children* 63 (4): 30–36.

Kissel, B.T. 2008. "Apples on Train Tracks: Observing Young Children Reenvision Their Writing." *Young Children* 63 (2): 26–32.

Klefstad, J.M., & K.C. Martinez. 2013. "Promoting Young Children's Cultural Awareness and Appreciation Through Multicultural Books." *Young Children* 68 (5): 74–81.

Kliewer, C. 2008. *Seeing All Kids as Readers: A New Vision for Literacy in the Inclusive Early Childhood Classroom*. Baltimore: Brookes.

Knopf, H.T., & H.M. Brown. 2009. "Lap Reading With Kindergartners: Nurturing Literacy Skills and So Much More." *Young Children* 64 (5): 80–87.

Lacina, J., & R. Stetson. 2013. "Using Children's Literature to Support Positive Behaviors." *Young Children* 68 (5): 34–41.

Lee, S. 2006. "Using Children's Texts to Communicate With Parents of English-Language Learners." *Young Children* 61 (5): 18–25.

Makin, L., C.J. Diaz, & C. McLachlan, eds. 2007. *Literacies in Childhood: Changing Views, Challenging Practice*. 2nd ed. Marrickville, Australia: MacLennan & Petty.

Mankiw, S., & J. Strasser. 2013. "Tender Topics: Exploring Sensitive Issues With Pre-K Through First Grade Children Through Read-Alouds." Expanded version. *Young Children* 68 (1): 84–89. www.naeyc.org/yc/article/tender_topics_exploring_sensitive_issues_mankiw_strasser.

Martin, L.E., & S. Thacker. 2009. "Teaching the Writing Process in Primary Grades: One Teacher's Approach." *Young Children* 64 (4): 30–35.

McNair, J.C. 2007. "Say My Name, Say My Name! Using Children's Names to Enhance Early Literacy Development." *Young Children* 62 (5): 84–89.

McNair, J.C. 2012. "Poems About Sandwich Cookies, Jelly, and Chocolate: Poetry in K–3 Classrooms." *Young Children* 67 (4): 94–100.

Meller, W.B., D. Richardson, & J.A. Hatch. 2009. "Using Read-Alouds With Critical Literacy Literature in K–3 Classrooms." Of Primary Interest. *Young Children* 64 (6): 76–78. www.naeyc.org/files/yc/file/200911/PrimaryInterestWeb1109.pdf.

NAEYC. 1995. *Responding to Linguistic and Cultural Diversity: Recommendations for Effective Early Childhood Education.* Position statement. Washington, DC: NAEYC. www.naeyc.org/positionstatements/linguistic.

NAEYC. 2007. "Beyond the Library Corner: Incorporating Books Throughout the Curriculum." Cluster theme. *Young Children* 62 (3). www.naeyc.org/yc/pastissues/2007/may.

NAEYC. 2007. "Teaching and Learning About Writing." Cluster theme. *Young Children* 62 (1). www.naeyc.org/yc/pastissues/2007/january.

NAEYC. 2009. "Teaching and Learning About Literacy." Cluster theme. *Young Children* 64 (1). www.naeyc.org/yc/pastissues/2009/january.

NAEYC. 2011. "Supporting the Many Ways Children Communicate." Cluster theme. *Young Children* 66 (2). www.naeyc.org/yc/pastissues/2011/march.

NAEYC. 2013. "Supporting Dual Language Learners and Their Families." Cluster theme. *Young Children* 68 (1). www.naeyc.org/yc/pastissues/2013/march.

NAEYC. Forthcoming. "Language and Literacy." Cluster theme. *Young Children* 69 (3). www.naeyc.org/yc/pastissues/2014/july.

NAEYC & International Reading Association (IRA). 1998. *Learning to Read and Write: Developmentally Appropriate Practices for Young Children.* Joint position statement. Washington, DC: NAEYC. www.naeyc.org/positionstatements/learning_readwrite.

Nemeth, K.N. 2009. "Meeting the Home Language Mandate: Practical Strategies for All Classrooms." *Young Children* 64 (2): 36–42.

Nemeth, K.N. 2012. *Basics of Supporting Dual Language Learners: An Introduction for Educators of Children From Birth Through Age 8.* Washington, DC: NAEYC.

Nemeth, K.N., & V. Erdosi. 2012. "Enhancing Practice With Infants and Toddlers From Diverse Language and Cultural Backgrounds." *Young Children* 67 (4): 49–57.

Paciga, K.A., J.L. Hoffman, & W.H. Teale. 2011. "The National Early Literacy Panel and Preschool Literacy Instruction: Green Lights, Caution Lights, and Red Lights." Viewpoint. *Young Children* 66 (6): 50–57.

Patè, M. 2009. "Language and Social Development in a Multilingual Classroom: A Dinosaur Project Enriched With Block Play." *Young Children* 64 (4): 12–19.

Roberts, S.K., & P.A. Crawford. 2008. "Real Life Calls for Real Books: Literature to Help Children Cope With Family Stressors." *Young Children* 63 (5): 12–17.

Saçkes, M., K.C. Trundle, & L.M. Flevares. 2009. "Using Children's Books to Teach Inquiry Skills." *Young Children* 64 (6): 24–26.

Santos, R.M., A. Fettig, & L. Shaffer. 2012. "Helping Families Connect Early Literacy With Social-Emotional Development." *Young Children* 67 (2): 88–93.

Schickedanz, J.A. 2008. *Increasing the Power of Instruction: Integration of Language, Literacy, and Math Across the Preschool Day.* Washington, DC: NAEYC.

Schickedanz, J.A., & M.F. Collins. 2013. *So Much More Than the ABCs: The Early Phases of Reading and Writing.* Washington, DC: NAEYC.

Shanahan, T., & C.J. Lonigan. 2013. *Early Childhood Literacy: The National Early Literacy Panel and Beyond.* Baltimore: Brookes.

Shedd, M.K., & N.K. Duke. 2008. "The Power of Planning: Developing Effective Read-Alouds." Research to Practice. *Young Children* 63 (6): 22–27. www.naeyc.org/files/yc/file/200811/BTJReadingAloud.pdf.

Soundy, C.S., & Y.H. Lee. 2013. "A Medley of Pictures and Patterns in Children's Drawings." *Young Children* 68 (2): 70–77. www.naeyc.org/yc/article/a_medley_of_pictures_and_patterns.

Souto-Manning, M. 2010. "Family Involvement: Challenges to Consider, Strengths to Build On." *Young Children* 65 (2): 82–88.

Stribling, S.M., & S.M. Kraus. 2007. "Content and Mechanics: Understanding First Grade Writers." *Voices of Practitioners* 2 (2): 1–17. www.naeyc.org/files/naeyc/file/vop/VoicesStriblingKraus%281%29.pdf.

Strickland, D.S., & S. Riley-Ayers. 2007. *Literacy Leadership in Early Childhood: The Essential Guide.* New York: Teachers College Press; Washington, DC: NAEYC.

Teachout, C., & A. Bright. 2007. "Reading the Pictures: A Missing Piece of the Literacy Puzzle." Teachers on Teaching. *Young Children* 62 (4): 106–7.

Thompson, S.C. 2005. *Children as Illustrators: Making Meaning Through Art and Language.* Washington, DC: NAEYC.

Whitin, D.J., & M. Piwko. 2008. "Mathematics and Poetry: The Right Connections." *Young Children* 63 (2): 34–39. www.naeyc.org/files/yc/file/200803/BTJ_Whitin.pdf.

Yopp, H.K., & R.H. Yopp. 2009. "Phonological Awareness Is Child's Play!" Expanded version. *Young Children* 64 (1): 12–21. www.naeyc.org/files/yc/file/200901/BTJPhonologicalAwareness.pdf.

Other Articles, Books, and Additional Resources

Babies. 2010. Directed by Thomas Balmès. Universal City, CA: Focus Features. www.focusfeatures.com/babies.

Bainer, C.C., & G.E. Myers. 2010. *Literacy in the Preschool Years: A Play Based Approach.* DVD & study guide. Oakland, CA: Blue Skies for Children.

Ballantyne, K.G., A.R. Sanderman, & J. Levy. 2008. *Educating English Language Learners: Building Teacher Capacity.* Roundtable report. Washington, DC: National Clearinghouse for English Language Acquisition. www.ncela.us/files/rcd/BE024215/EducatingELLsBuildingTeacherCa.pdf.

Barclay, K., L. Stewart, & D.M. Lee. 2014. *The Everything Guide to Informational Texts, K–2: Best Texts, Best Practices.* Thousand Oaks, CA: Corwin.

Beaty, J.J. 2012. *50 Early Childhood Literacy Strategies.* 3rd ed. Upper Saddle River, NJ: Prentice Hall.

Beaty, J.J., & L. Pratt. 2013. *Early Literacy in Preschool and Kindergarten: A Multicultural Perspective.* 3rd ed. Upper Saddle River, NJ: Pearson Prentice Hall.

Bennett-Armistead, V.S., N.K. Duke, & A.M. Moses. 2005. *Literacy and the Youngest Learner: Best Practices for Educators of Children From Birth to 5.* Teaching Resources Series. New York: Scholastic. Available from NAEYC.

Bos, B. 1987. *Before the Basics: Creating Conversations With Children*. Roseville, CA: Turn the Page Press.

Boushey, G., & J. Moser. 2014. *The Daily 5: Fostering Literacy in the Elementary Grades*. 2nd ed. Portland, ME: Stenhouse.

Castro, D.C., L.M. Espinosa, & M.M. Páez. 2011. "Defining and Measuring Quality in Early Childhood Practices That Promote Dual Language Learners' Development and Learning." Chap. 11 in *Quality Measurement in Early Childhood Settings*, eds. M. Zaslow, I. Martinez-Beck, K. Tout, & T. Halle, 257–80. Baltimore: Brookes.

Castro, D.C., C. Gillanders, M. Machado-Casas, & V. Buysse. 2006. *Nuestros Niños Early Language and Literacy Program*. Chapel Hill: University of North Carolina, FPG Child Development Institute.

Castro, D.C., M.M. Páez, D.K. Dickinson, & E. Frede. 2011. "Promoting Language and Literacy in Young Dual Language Learners: Research, Practice, and Policy." *Child Development Perspectives* 5 (1): 15–21.

Collins, M.F. 2010. "ELL Preschoolers' English Vocabulary Acquisition From Storybook Reading." *Early Childhood Research Quarterly* 25 (1): 84–97.

Cooper, P.M. 2009. *The Classrooms All Young Children Need: Lessons in Teaching From Vivian Paley*. Chicago: University of Chicago Press.

Cremin, T., J. Swann, R. Flewitt, D. Faulkner, & N. Kucirkova. 2013. "Evaluation Report of MakeBelieve Arts Helicopter Technique of Storytelling and Story Acting." London: Make-Believe Arts. www.makebelievearts.co.uk/docs/Helicopter-Technique-Evaluation.pdf.

Cunningham, A., & R. Shagoury. 2005. *Starting With Comprehension: Reading Strategies for the Youngest Learners*. Portland, ME: Stenhouse.

Daniels, H., & E. Daniels. 2013. *The Best-Kept Teaching Secret: How Written Conversations Engage Kids, Activate Learning, and Grow Fluent Writers, K–12*. Thousand Oaks, CA: Corwin.

DEC (Council for Exceptional Children Division for Early Childhood). 2010. "Responsiveness to ALL Children, Families, and Professionals: Integrating Cultural and Linguistic Diversity Into Policy and Practice." Position statement. Missoula, MT: DEC. http://dec.membershipsoftware.org/files/Position%20 Statement%20and%20Papers/Position%20Statement_ Cultural%20and%20Linguistic%20Diversity.pdf.

Dennis, K., & T. Azpiri. 2005. *Sign to Learn: American Sign Language in the Early Childhood Classroom*. St. Paul, MN: Redleaf.

Dickinson, D.K., & M.V. Porche. 2011. "Relation Between Language Experiences in Preschool Classrooms and Children's Kindergarten and Fourth-Grade Language and Reading Abilities." *Child Development* 82 (3): 870–86.

Diller, D. 2008. *Spaces and Places: Designing Classrooms for Literacy*. Portland, ME: Stenhouse.

Dorfman, L.R., & R. Cappelli. 2007. *Mentor Texts: Teaching Writing Through Children's Literature, K–6*. Portland, ME: Stenhouse.

Dorfman, L.R., & R. Cappelli. 2009. *Nonfiction Mentor Texts: Teaching Informational Writing Through Children's Literature, K–8*. Portland, ME: Stenhouse.

Dorfman, L.R., & R. Cappelli. 2012. *Poetry Mentor Texts: Making Reading and Writing Connections, K–8*. Portland, ME: Stenhouse.

Dorn, L.J., & T. Jones. 2012. *Apprenticeship in Literacy: Transitions Across Reading and Writing, K–4*. 2nd ed. Portland, ME: Stenhouse.

Dragan, P.B. 2005. *A How-to Guide for Teaching English Language Learners in the Primary Classroom*. Portsmouth, NH: Heinemann. Available from NAEYC.

Dyson, A.H. 2013. *ReWRITING the Basics: Literacy Learning in Children's Cultures*. New York: Teachers College Press.

Elliott, E.M., & C.B. Olliff. 2008. "Developmentally Appropriate Emergent Literacy Activities for Young Children: Adapting the Early Literacy and Learning Model." *Early Childhood Education Journal* 35 (6): 551–56.

Enz, B.J., & L.M. Morrow. 2009. *Assessing Preschool Literacy Development: Informal and Formal Measures to Guide Instruction*. Newark, DE: International Reading Association. Available from NAEYC.

Epstein, A.S. 2012. *Language, Literacy, and Communication*. Ypsilanti, MI: HighScope.

Espinosa, L.M. 2013. "PreK–3rd: Challenging Common Myths About Dual Language Learners—An Update to the Seminal 2008 Report." *Policy to Action Brief* 10. Foundation for Child Development. www.fcd-us.org/sites/default/files/ Challenging%20Common%20Myths%20Update.pdf.

Gadzikowski, A. 2007. *Story Dictation: A Guide for Early Childhood Professionals*. St. Paul, MN: Redleaf Press.

Goldenberg, C., J. Hicks, & I. Lit. 2013. "Dual Language Learners: Effective Instruction in Early Childhood." *American Educator* 37 (2): 26–29. www.aft.org/pdfs/americaneducator/ summer2013/Goldenberg_Hicks_Lit.pdf.

Goldstein, B.A., ed. 2012. *Bilingual Language Development and Disorders in Spanish-English Speakers*. 2nd ed. Baltimore: Brookes.

Gonzalez-Mena, J. 2007. *Diversity in Early Care and Education: Honoring Differences*. 5th ed. New York: McGraw Hill.

Haraksin-Probst, L., J. Hutson-Brandhagen, & P.S. Weikart. 2008. *Making Connections: Movement, Music, and Literacy*. Ypsilanti, MI: HighScope.

Herrera, S.G., & K.G. Murray. 2005. *Mastering ESL and Bilingual Methods: Differentiated Instruction for Culturally and Linguistically Diverse Students*. Boston: Allyn and Bacon.

Herrera, S.G., D.R. Perez, S.K. Kavimandan, & S. Wessels. 2013. *Accelerating Literacy for Diverse Learners: Strategies for the Common Core Classroom, K–8*. New York: Teachers College Press.

Hohmann, M., & J. Tangorra. 2007. *Let's Talk Literacy: Practical Readings for Preschool Teachers*. Ypsilanti, MI: HighScope.

Howes, C., J.T. Downer, & R.C. Pianta. 2011. *Dual Language Learners in the Early Childhood Classroom*. Baltimore: Brookes. Available from NAEYC.

Hynes-Berry. M. 2012. *Don't Leave the Story in the Book: Using Literature to Guide Inquiry in Early Childhood Classrooms*. New York: Teachers College Press. Available from NAEYC.

Im, J.H., C.A. Osborn, S.Y. Sánchez, & E.K. Thorp. 2007. *Cradling Literacy: Building Teachers' Skills to Nurture Early Language and Literacy From Birth to 5*. A ZERO TO THREE Training Curriculum. Washington, DC: ZERO TO THREE.

Israel, S.E. 2008. *Early Reading First and Beyond: A Guide to Building Early Literacy Skills*. Thousand Oaks, CA: Corwin.

Jalongo, M.R. 2013. *Early Childhood Language Arts*. 6th ed. Boston: Allyn & Bacon.

Johnson, D. 2014. *Reading, Writing, and Literacy 2.0: Teaching with Online Texts, Tools, and Resources, K–8*. New York: Teachers College Press.

Kovach, B., & D. Da Ros-Voseles. 2008. *Being With Babies: Understanding and Responding to the Infants in Your Care*. Silver Spring, MD: Gryphon House.

Kuby, C.R. 2013. *Critical Literacy in the Early Childhood Classroom: Unpacking Histories, Unlearning Privilege*. Language and Literacy Series. New York: Teachers College Press.

Kuhl, P. 2010. "The Linguistic Genius of Babies." Filmed October 2010. TED video, 10:18. Posted February 2011. www.ted.com/talks/patricia_kuhl_the_linguistic_genius_of_babies.

Lindfors, J.W. 2008. *Children's Language: Connecting Reading, Writing, and Talk.* Language and Literacy Series. New York: Teachers College Press.

Lugo-Neris, M.J., C.W. Jackson, & H. Goldstein. 2010. "Facilitating Vocabulary Acquisition of Young English Language Learners." *Language, Speech, and Hearing Services in Schools* 41 (3): 314–27.

Matera, C. 2011. "Supporting Early Writing in Dual Language Head Start Classrooms." *NHSA Dialog* 14 (3): 147–50.

Meier, D.R. 2004. *The Young Child's Memory for Words: Developing First and Second Language and Literacy.* New York: Teachers College Press. Available from NAEYC.

Meier, D.R. 2011. *Teaching Children to Write: Constructing Meaning and Mastering Mechanics.* New York: Teachers College Press. Available from NAEYC.

Morrow, L.M. 2014. *Literacy Development in the Early Years: Helping Children Read and Write.* 7th ed. Essex, UK: Pearson.

National Early Literacy Panel. 2008. *Developing Early Literacy: Report of the National Early Literacy Panel.* Washington, DC: National Institute for Literacy. www.nichd.nih.gov/publications/pubs/documents/NELPReport09.pdf.

Nemeth, K. 2009. *Many Languages, One Classroom: Teaching Dual and English Language Learners.* Silver Spring, MD: Gryphon House. Available from NAEYC.

Nemeth, K. 2012. *Many Languages, Building Connections: Supporting Infants and Toddlers Who Are Dual Language Learners.* Silver Spring, MD: Gryphon House. Available from NAEYC.

Neuman, S.B., & D.K. Dickinson, eds. 2011. *Handbook of Early Literacy Research.* Vol. 3. New York: Guilford.

Neuman, S.B., & L.B. Gambrell, eds. 2013. *Quality Reading Instruction in the Age of Common Core Standards.* Newark, DE: International Reading Association.

Neuman, S.B., & K. Roskos, With T. Wright & L. Lenhart. 2007. *Nurturing Knowledge: Building a Foundation for School Success by Linking Early Literacy to Math, Science, Art, and Social Studies.* New York: Scholastic. Available from NAEYC.

Neuman, S.B., & T.S. Wright. 2013. *All About Words: Increasing Vocabulary in the Common Core Classroom, PreK–2.* Common Core State Standards for Literacy Series. New York: Teachers College Press.

NGA (National Governors Association Center for Best Practices). 2013. *A Governor's Guide to Early Literacy: Getting All Students Reading by Third Grade.* Washington, DC: NGA. www.nga.org/files/live/sites/NGA/files/pdf/2013/1310NGAEarlyLiteracyReportWeb.pdf.

Nicolopoulou, A., J. McDowell, & C. Brockmeyer. 2006. "Narrative Play and Emergent Literacy: Storytelling and Story-Acting Meet Journal Writing." Chap. 7 in *Play = Learning: How Play Motivates and Enhances Children's Cognitive and Social-Emotional Growth*, eds. D.G. Singer, R.M. Golinkoff, & K. Hirsh-Pasek, 124–44. New York: Oxford University Press.

Owocki, G. 2007. *Literate Days: Reading and Writing With Preschool and Primary Children.* Portsmouth, NH: Heinemann.

Paley, V.G. 1997. *The Girl With the Brown Crayon: How Children Use Stories to Shape Their Lives.* Cambridge, MA: Harvard University Press.

Palmer, S., & R. Bayley. 2005. *Early Literacy Fundamentals: A Balanced Approach to Language, Listening, and Literacy Skills, Ages 3 to 6.* Markham, ON: Pembroke.

Pandey, A. 2012. *Language Building Blocks: Essential Linguistics for Early Childhood Educators.* New York: Teachers College Press.

Parr, M., & T. Campbell. 2012. *Balanced Literacy Essentials: Weaving Theory Into Practice for Successful Instruction in Reading, Writing, and Talk.* Markham, ON: Pembroke.

Parsons, S. 2005. *First Grade Writers: Units of Study to Help Children Plan, Organize, and Structure Their Ideas.* Portsmouth, NH: Heinemann.

Passe, A.S. 2012. *Dual-Language Learners: Strategies for Teaching English.* St. Paul, MN: Redleaf.

Rosenkoetter, S.E., & J. Knapp-Philo, eds. 2006. *Learning to Read the World: Language and Literacy in the First Three Years.* Washington, DC: ZERO TO THREE.

Samson, J.F., & B.A. Collins. 2012. *Preparing All Teachers to Meet the Needs of English Language Learners: Applying Research to Policy and Practice for Teacher Effectiveness.* Washington, DC: Center for American Progress. www.americanprogress.org/issues/education/report/2012/04/30/11372/preparing-all-teachers-to-meet-the-needs-of-english-language-learners.

Samway, K.D. 2006. *When English Language Learners Write: Connecting Research to Practice, K–8.* Portsmouth, NH: Heinemann.

Schiller, P., & C. Willis. 2008. *Inclusive Literacy Lessons for Early Childhood.* Beltsville, MD: Gryphon House.

Segal Bardige, B.L., & M.M. Segal. 2005. *Building Literacy With Love: A Guide for Teachers and Caregivers of Children Birth Through Age 5.* Washington, DC: ZERO TO THREE.

Segal Bardige, B.L., & M.M. Segal. 2005. *Poems to Learn to Read By: Building Literacy With Love.* Washington, DC: ZERO TO THREE.

Seplocha, H., J. Jablon, & J. Strasser. 2007. *The Essential Literacy Workshop Book: 10 Complete Early Childhood Training Modules.* Beltsville, MD: Gryphon House.

Sipe, L.R. 2008. *Storytime: Young Children's Literacy Understanding in the Classroom.* Language and Literacy Series. New York: Teachers College Press.

Soderman, A.K., & P.E. Farrell. 2008. *Creating Literacy-Rich Preschools and Kindergartens.* Boston: Pearson.

Souto-Manning, M. 2013. *Multicultural Teaching in the Early Childhood Classroom: Approaches, Strategies, and Tools, Preschool–2nd Grade.* Early Childhood Education Series. New York: Teachers College Press; Washington, DC: Association for Childhood Education International.

Stahl, S.A., & W.E. Nagy. 2006. *Teaching Word Meanings.* Literacy Teaching Series. Mahwah, NJ: Erlbaum.

Tabors, P.O. 2008. *One Child, Two Languages: A Guide for Early Childhood Educators of Children Learning English as a Second Language.* 2nd ed. Baltimore: Brookes. Available from NAEYC.

Templeton, S. 2013. *Teaching Reading and Writing: The Developmental Approach.* Boston: Pearson.

Templeton, S., & K.M. Gehsmann. 2013. *Teaching Reading and Writing: The Developmental Approach.* Boston: Pearson.

TESOL (Teachers of English to Speakers of Other Languages). 2010. "Position Paper on Language and Literacy Development for Young English Language Learners (Ages 3–8)." Alexandria, VA: TESOL. www.tesol.org/docs/pdf/371.pdf?sfvrsn=2.

Tyner, B. 2009. *Small-Group Reading Instruction: A Differentiated Teaching Model for Beginning and Struggling Readers.* 2nd ed. Newark, DE: International Reading Association.

Vestergaard, H. 2005. *Weaving the Literacy Web: Creating Curriculum Based on Books Children Love.* St. Paul, MN: Redleaf Press.

Weitzman, E., & J. Greenberg. 2010. *ABC and Beyond: Building Emergent Literacy in Early Childhood Settings.* Toronto, ON: Hanen Centre. Available from NAEYC.

Wohlwend, K.E. 2013. *Literacy Playshop: New Literacies, Popular Media, and Play in the Early Childhood Classroom.* Language and Literacy Series. New York: Teachers College Press.

Zacarian, D. 2013. *Mastering Academic Language: A Framework for Supporting Student Achievement.* Thousand Oaks, CA: Corwin.

Zigler, E., D.G. Singer, & S.J. Bishop-Josef, eds. 2004. *Children's Play: The Roots of Reading.* Washington, DC: ZERO TO THREE.

Journal and Web Resources

Annenberg Learner—Part of the Annenberg Foundation, this website provides multimedia resources for K–12 teachers. Included are two video series focusing on literature and the language arts for grades K–2. www.learner.org

Becoming Bilingual—Actress Rita Moreno hosts this 30-minute PBS program that examines the challenges of teaching children a new language. The show visits six cities across the country to learn how schools are working to create bilingual readers. *Becoming Bilingual* is the seventh episode of the series *Launching Young Readers.* www.readingrockets.org/shows/launching/bilingual.

Boston Public Schools Early Childhood—This website hosts resources about the storytelling/story acting (ST/SA) program, including video examples of children engaging in ST/SA, a document listing how ST/SA meets NAEYC Early Childhood Program Standards, and strategies for supporting children with a range of abilities, needs, and proficiencies in English. http://bpsearlychildhood.weebly.com/guides.html

¡Colorín Colorado!—This bilingual (Spanish and English) website is for families and educators of dual language learners. It offers webcasts, newsletters, bilingual booklists, and research and reports about dual language learners and effective instruction. www.colorincolorado.org

The Cooperative Children's Book Center—Funded by the University of Wisconsin–Madison School of Education, this site provides resources focusing on children's literature. The site offers podcasts on selected books, booklists on a wide range of themes, including those aligned with the Common Core State Standards, and webcasts by a wide range of authors and artists. http://ccbc.education.wisc.edu

The International Children's Digital Library—This organization's goal is to build a collection of outstanding children's literature from around the world. Visitors can use the site's search engine to find online books by age group and language. A Teacher Trainer Manual offers tips about using the search engine and building on book content in the classroom. http://en.childrenslibrary.org

The International Reading Association—This organization supports literacy professionals who serve readers of all ages. It offers online resources on a variety of literacy topics, including reading lists and units and lesson plans. The association publishes *The Reading Teacher*, a monthly journal, from September to May for educators who work with children up to age 12. www.reading.org

Journal of Early Childhood Literacy—Published quarterly, the JECL emphasizes research about the nature, function, and use of literacy in early childhood. http://ecl.sagepub.com

A Mighty Girl—Embracing a mission of empowering young girls through literacy, this website has thematically organized booklist recommendations, tips for creating book clubs, family resources such as information about bullying, and links to research on gender issues. www.amightygirl.com

National Center on Cultural and Linguistic Responsiveness—NCCLR provides the Head Start community and others with research-based resources, practices, and strategies to support diverse children and families. The site includes webcasts, a bilingual glossary, a program checklist, hands-on strategies in Quick Guides for Teachers, and other resources. www.eclkc.ohs.acf.hhs.gov/hslc/tta-system/cultural-linguistic/center

National Writing Project—This organization is a network of writing project sites across all 50 states, the District of Columbia, Puerto Rico, and the US Virgin Islands. Project sites partner with area school districts to offer high-quality professional development programs for educators centered on children's writing. The site includes a list of projects organized by location as well as resources on a variety of topics related to supporting young children's writing. www.nwp.org

Read Write Think—In partnership with the National Council of Teachers of English (NCTE) and the International Reading Association (IRA), this website provides educators with classroom materials, activities for grades K–12, professional development tools, and training videos. It also offers after-school resources for families. http://readwritethink.org

Reading Is Fundamental (RIF)—This organization focuses on helping children learn to read and write—providing millions of new, free books to children across the United States. The site offers free articles for teachers and families about a variety of literacy topics, booklists, multicultural literacy resources, and activities for children. www.rif.org

Reading Rockets—This project brings research-based strategies to educators, families, and others involved in helping children learn to read. The site includes resources for teaching reading and helping struggling readers, such as short articles and videos, professional development webcasts, tips for first-year teachers, and teaching strategies that align with Common Core State Standards. www.readingrockets.org

Reflecting, Discussing, and Exploring
Questions and Follow-Up Activities

Sue Mankiw

The articles in *Spotlight on Young Children: Exploring Language and Literacy* represent just a small selection of the many valuable resources for early childhood educators interested in supporting the language and literacy development of young children. We hope these articles provide ideas for teacher educators, students in early childhood professional preparation programs, early childhood teachers taking part in professional development, and others seeking to broaden their understanding of language and literacy development in the early years.

To help readers review and expand on ideas, we have developed this study guide—a series of questions and follow-up activities. First, we invite you to think about your own early experiences with language and literacy. We then ask you to make connections between your early experiences and strategies for promoting children's language and literacy skills. Specific questions and suggested activities related to each article then follow. Finally, general questions about curriculum, teaching practices, resources, and next steps can help you pull together concepts and teaching strategies.

A. Recalling Your Own Early Experiences

1. What were your favorite books as a child? How did you discover these books and why did they interest you? What did you like to draw and write about? Who or what inspired your emergent writing?

Sue Mankiw, EdD, is an assistant professor and director of the early childhood teaching program at William Paterson University in Wayne, New Jersey. Her research and teaching focus on using read-alouds to support the exploration of diversity and equity issues with preservice teachers and young children. Sue is a consulting editor for *Young Children*.

2. What do you recall about your early experiences learning new vocabulary, reading, and writing? Who or what was most helpful in promoting your language skills? In what ways did the adults in your life support the development of these skills? What additional supports could they have provided to better promote skill development?

3. Many of the articles in this series address the language and literacy development of dual language learners. If you grew up speaking more than one language, what do you recall about your early language and literacy experiences in school? What were the challenges? What experiences were most beneficial?

B. Expanding on Each Article

"The Daily Dozen: Strategies for Enhancing Social Communication of Infants With Language Delays" / Nancy Stockall and Lindsay R. Dennis

The authors describe 12 intentional early language strategies that are appropriate for all infants but are critical when supporting infants who have developmental delays.

1. Discuss with a partner which of the 12 strategies you have already used with infants in your setting or with those in your family or community. Discuss how these infants have responded to the strategies. Then consider your past interactions with an infant who had suspected or identified developmental delays. In terms of social communication, how were these interactions different from your interactions with infants with no delays? How were your interactions similar?

2. The film *Babies* (2010; directed by Thomas Balmès) chronicles the first year of life for four babies, born in San Francisco, Tokyo, Mongolia, and Namibia. Download and watch the beginning portions of the film. Using the daily dozen lan-

Spotlight on Young Children: Exploring Language and Literacy

guage strategies as a guide, notice the early social interactions and exchanges between each infant and the adults in his or her environment. Given the distinctly diverse home settings, what similarities and differences do you see in the interactions between adults and infants? How do the adults and infants initiate communication with each other? How do they respond to each other? Watch the rest of the film. How do these early communications contribute to the infants' overall language development? If you were asked to make a list of language goals for an infant's first year, what would you include and why?

3. When teachers and families gain a richer understanding of how early language and social skills develop, the goals of the daily dozen for infants with developmental delays become more evident. Why is it especially important to respond to the nonverbal communication of an infant with developmental delays?

"What Do We Mean by Reading Readiness?" / Nikki Darling-Kuria

The author describes strategies for communicating and working with families to promote developmentally appropriate ways to support infants' and toddlers' literacy development.

4. Reflect on a time when you did not agree with a family's request based on your knowledge of children's development and developmentally appropriate practices. How did you approach the family? How did they respond? After reading this article, what would you do differently? How do you think the family would have responded to your new approach?

5. Consider the ethical dimensions of the scenario in this article—the teacher's desire to support families' goals for their children and her obligation to support children in developmentally appropriate ways. Review NAEYC's Code of Ethical Conduct, which offers guidelines for responsible behavior and sets forth a common basis for resolving ethical dilemmas that early educators may face (visit www.naeyc.org/positionstatements/ethical_conduct). Select those passages that could facilitate a teacher's decision about how to solve this ethical dilemma.

6. In addition to having conferences with families, what other ways can teachers help families understand the connection between early language development and reading readiness? What do you already know about the home literacy practices of the families in your program, and how can you find out more? How can you use that knowledge to foster children's learning in developmentally appropriate ways in your setting and when children are at home with their families?

"Sagacious, Sophisticated, and Sedulous: The Importance of Discussing 50-Cent Words With Preschoolers" / Molly F. Collins

The author shares how early oral language skills predict later reading comprehension. The article offers ways to strengthen preschoolers' vocabularies by initiating conversations about high-level vocabulary words that come up during storybook readings, conversations, and classroom activities.

7. Did you encounter any new words when reading the article? If so, how did you figure out their meanings?

8. Choose a piece of children's literature that includes sophisticated vocabulary. Mark the passages that contain "50-cent words." Work with a partner to create a plan for introducing, explaining, and discussing these new words with children. Reflect on how you think children might respond. Then read the book aloud to children, implement your plan, record and review children's responses, and revise your plan as needed for future read-aloud sessions.

9. In the graphic "Using *Persevere* Across Multiple Contexts," the author illustrates opportunities for teachers to support children's understanding of new, sophisticated words across several experiences throughout the day. Select a sophisticated word from a book you recently read to children and create a similar graphic. Then implement the strategies suggested in the article and reflect on the children's responses.

"Helping Children Prepare for Writing: Developing Fine Motor Skills" / J. Michelle Huffman and Callie Fortenberry

The authors explain the four developmental stages of fine motor development and describe engaging activities that help young children prepare for and practice writing.

10. What is the relationship between the stages of fine motor development and the stages of writing development?

11. The authors note that "teachers can alleviate frustration and nurture emerging fine motor skills by providing materials and activities that support differentiated instruction for each stage of physical development." Assess your classroom. Using the activity table provided in the article, identify activities in your classroom that address the four stages of fine motor development—whole arm, whole hand, pincher, and pincer coordination. How might you integrate additional fine motor activities into existing learning center experiences?

12. Develop a plan for sharing with families information about children's fine motor development and ways to support it at home. For example, discuss the article with families, provide the article ideas in a newsletter or blog, share information during parent meetings, and display a documentation board with photographs and explanations of what children are practicing. Promote family engagement by asking families to donate materials that support this development (see "Activities That Promote Fine Motor Development" on p. 24 for ideas about items to request).

"Using Photo-Narration to Support the Language Development of All Learners" / Barbara A. Marinak, Martha J. Strickland, and Jane Blakely Keat

The authors describe preschool teachers' use of the language experience approach (LEA), in which children narrate stories about photographs they took at home. These meaningful experiences promote child-teacher communication and give teachers insights about the children and their families.

13. Practice using the photo-narration approach with a colleague. Bring in a photograph from your personal life, and ask a colleague to record your story as you describe the picture. Have your colleague read back your narration. Based on your photo-narration, what concepts might you discuss? What vocabulary words come to mind? How does this experience support meaningful communication between you and your colleague?

14. Consider how the children in your setting might respond to photo-narration. How could it enhance their literacy skills? In what ways could it promote your relationships with them?

15. For further discussion, read the seminal work about Mexican and Yaqui families titled *Funds of Knowledge for Teaching: Using a Qualitative Approach to Connect Homes and Classrooms* (L.C. Moll, C. Amanti, D. Neff, & N. Gonzalez, 1992, *Theory Into Practice* (21) 2: 132–41). This article is available online at www.sonoma.edu/users/f/filp/ed415/moll.pdf. Discuss what happens when teachers find opportunities to learn about and make connections to the valuable knowledge children already possess from their home lives. How do you include families' funds of knowledge in your curriculum?

"Storybook Reading for Young Dual Language Learners" / Cristina Gillanders and Dina C. Castro

This article describes how reading storybooks aloud can promote the early language and literacy development of preschool dual language learners. Strategies include those for English-speaking teachers.

16. With a partner, review and discuss the sample storybook-reading lesson plan in the article, which centers on the book *La Cucaracha Martina: A Caribbean Folktale* by Daniel Moreton. How do the strategies in the lesson contribute to the language development of all learners, especially dual language learners?

17. Gather a variety of books for the classroom library that are available in English and the home languages of the dual language learners in your classroom. Work with at least one colleague to create a lesson plan focusing on one of these books, using the strategies described in the article. Ask a colleague to observe and record you implementing the plan in your setting. Review together how the children responded, what they learned, and how you can extend this learning in the future.

"Vivian Paley's Storytelling/Story Acting Comes to the Boston Public Schools" / Ben Mardell, Marina Boni, and Jason Sachs

The work of well-known storyteller and author Vivian Paley provides the foundation for storytelling/story acting (ST/SA) in 50 Boston kindergarten classrooms. The authors describe the process of ST/SA, skills it promotes, and specific strategies to use with dual language learners and children with special needs.

18. The authors note, "The core components of storytelling/story acting are straightforward—take a story and act it out." Consider how you could make time to use this approach in your setting. How do you think children would respond? How could you use this approach to build on the unique interests and skills of the children in your setting?

19. Visit the Boston Public Schools' storytelling website, listed in the article. View the video examples of ST/SA in action. Work with a colleague to develop a plan to use this approach in your setting. Document the implementation—what do teachers and children do? What happens as a result? After implementing the approach for at least three weeks, review and discuss the documentation with your colleague. With two children in mind, make a list of the language and literacy skills they gained or developed through ST/SA.

"Language to Language: Nurturing Writing Development in Multilingual Classrooms" / Ruth Shagoury

The author describes how to create a classroom environment that nurtures the writing development of dual language learners and what teachers can do to support kindergarten children's prewriting and writing skills.

20. Write down three ideas you learned about the writing processes of young children who are dual language learners. What do you need to apply these strategies in your own setting? Try them out and document how children respond.

21. Reflect on the following quote from the article and discuss it with at least one colleague or peer: " . . . children need the chance to explore how written language works in different situations, continually trying out their hypotheses." In what ways do you offer children such opportunities? What could you do differently to better support children's written communication?

22. How much do you know about the symbols, sequence, and direction of writing systems in different languages? Consider how you could build knowledge on this topic and feel more confident about addressing diverse writing systems. For instance, invite children's families to share their knowledge about speaking and writing in different languages, or consult with other community members who have this expertise. Also look for

resources. For example, to learn more about written Chinese, consult a resource such as "Chinese Preschool Children's Literacy Development: From Emergent to Conventional Writing" (L. Chan, C.Z. Juan, & C.L. Foon, 2008, *Early Years: An International Research Journal* 28 (2): 135–48).

"Let's Look in a Book! Using Nonfiction Reference Materials With Young Children" / Nell K. Duke

This article explains the benefits of using nonfiction reference materials to develop first-graders' literacy skills. By encouraging children to use these materials to find answers to their questions and by integrating reference materials into everyday activities, teachers also build children's knowledge of the world.

23. The article provides many examples of common nonfiction reference materials, such as information books, field guides, dictionaries, weather reports, periodicals, and record books. Assess your classroom. What nonfiction reference materials are you currently using with children? How do children respond to these materials? What reference materials would you like to add?

24. Choose a few new reference materials such as those described in the article and incorporate them into everyday classroom activities. For example, if children have been interested in the birds that visit the feeder outside the classroom window, introduce a bird field guide and discuss with children how to use it to identify birds. Observe and record children's responses to the new resources. Did the materials spark children's interest? What new ideas and vocabulary words did children encounter? What additional questions did children raise? How did you help children gain new knowledge using the nonfiction texts?

"First Grade Writers Revisit Their Work" / Jane A. Hansen

The author describes a community of children as they gain language and literacy skills through writers' workshops across the curriculum. The children evaluate their own work, then review and revise their text and illustrations to ensure that their messages are clear.

25. The author mentions that children's conversations with each other as they write contributes to their feeling of community, a necessary ingredient for a classroom of writers. In what ways can social interactions contribute to children's emergent writing?

26. In the article, what specific strategies does the teacher use to encourage children's reading and writing skills? Which of these strategies might you incorporate in your setting? For example, how could you encourage daily writing across the curriculum? How do you think the children in your setting would respond?

"'Snow on My Eyelashes'—Language Awareness Through Age-Appropriate Poetry Experiences" / Charles A. Elster

The author demonstrates how poetry promotes first and second grade children's language awareness by highlighting two teachers' classroom experiences.

27. How does reading, rereading, performing, and discussing poetry promote young readers' and writers' language awareness? How can teachers connect poetry experiences to children's cultural backgrounds?

28. Select a favorite poem, or one the author suggests on page 80, and develop and implement a plan for reading and discussing it with young children. For example, develop open-ended questions about the poem to encourage discussion, determine what poetic elements and aesthetic qualities you will bring to children's attention, and identify potential ways children can make text-to-life connections.

"Young Girls Discovering Their Voice With Literacy and Readers Theater" / Debby Zambo

This article describes how literacy-based activities such as Readers Theater can expand second grade girls' views of gender roles, helping them develop more positive self-concepts and better relationships with peers.

29. What were your earliest lessons about gender roles? How has your thinking about these roles stayed the same or changed over time? How does your current view influence your interactions with children and families?

30. How do you typically respond to bullying and/or relational aggression among young children? What has worked well? What challenges do you still face? How do you think the children you teach would respond to the strategies the author presents?

31. What does research say about how media role models affect young children's development? What negative impacts can they have on children? What positive impacts can they have? Work with a colleague to find examples of television shows, commercials, magazine ads, or children's books with girl characters. How are the girls portrayed? What are their roles? Discuss why you think the representation is accurate, fair, or biased.

"Every Language Is Special: Promoting Dual Language Learning in Multicultural Primary Schools"/ María Paula Ghiso

The author writes about a summer program for second- and third-graders in a school district that serves children from 69 countries. She describes ways to support children's acquisition of English skills and to value and build on children's home languages and cultures.

32. What do you know about the cultural and linguistic backgrounds of the children in your setting? How can you build on the knowledge and experiences of children and families in your everyday curriculum?

33. Mrs. Rangan successfully tapped district resources to advocate for students and cultivate relationships with families. How do you currently use home–school networks? After reading this article, what new ideas do you want to try? Using the strategies described in the article, create an environment that supports and values multilingual literacies. For example, invite children to tell family stories and to share their own immigration histories. Infuse the curriculum with multicultural and bilingual children's literature. Encourage children to use their home languages in their writing.

C. Making Connections

Consider the Big Picture

1. In your view, what are the three most important themes or recurring key ideas throughout the articles? If possible, compare your choices with those of others.

2. What did you learn about teaching strategies for children from various cultures and who speak different languages? Why is it important to incorporate children's cultures and languages into the curriculum? Consider the importance of supporting children with various skills and abilities. How do the approaches discussed in the articles help educators meet the needs of individual children? How could teachers adapt these strategies to support children with special needs? How can you apply what you learned to the children in your program?

3. By listening to stories, children learn about written syntax and vocabulary and develop phonological awareness and concepts of print—all of which support literacy skill development. Several articles discuss reading aloud as a starting point for introducing new and advanced vocabulary words. What did you learn about using vocabulary words that are just beyond the understanding of young learners?

4. What are the three most important things you learned about the development of emergent writing? What role does dictation play in the development of writing skills? What role does the development of fine motor skills play? What does a differentiated approach for teaching writing look like?

Examine Curriculum Goals and Expected Outcomes

5. Read NAEYC's position statement titled *Responding to Linguistic and Cultural Diversity: Recommendations for Effective Early Childhood Education* (1995), which stresses the importance of valuing the home languages and cultures of dual language learners. (This document can be accessed at www.naeyc.org/positionstatements/linguistic.) Select three quotes from the position statement to discuss with a group of colleagues or peers. How does the position statement support what you learned from the articles in this collection? How do your program practices align with NAEYC's position statement? What could you do differently to better support NAEYC's recommendations?

6. How does the content of the articles relate to your curriculum, the Common Core State Standards, state and local early learning standards, content standards, or other requirements applicable to your setting?

Use Reflection to Enhance Teaching Practices

7. Which ideas presented in the articles or raised in your discussions affirm your work with or on behalf of young children and families? Which ideas cause you to question your practices? What new approaches might you use to promote young children's language and literacy development? How do you think these changes would benefit children and families?

8. Several articles illustrate the connection between language and literacy and other content areas, such as social studies and the creative arts. They also illustrate connections with other developmental domains, such as social and emotional development and physical development. How do you use language and literacy to support other areas of learning and development? After reading these articles, what new approaches might you try?

9. Several authors emphasize the importance of having a keen sense of observation and of planning and documenting children's language and literacy activities. Develop a daily plan for observing, documenting, and reflecting on children's development. For example, decide when during the schedule you will observe children and what you will observe, such as their ability to answer their own questions by reading nonfiction resources. Determine how you will document children's progress (for example, with anecdotal notes, checklists, video clips, documentation boards, journals, and/or work samples). Decide how you will use your reflections about this documentation for planning. For example, after reviewing your notes, you may notice that several children are interested in the ladybugs they see on the playground and decide to add several books about insects to the classroom library.

Focus on Families and Communities

10. Discuss how children's language and literacy development is enhanced when teachers weave children's experiences and cultures into all aspects of the classroom environment and curriculum.

Work with a colleague to create a list of the materials, activities, and events that you could use to build on children's personal experiences and cultures.

11. Several articles discuss the importance of teachers partnering with families to support children's early language and literacy development. What new strategies for engaging families would you like to try after reading the articles?

12. Consider ways to encourage families of dual language learners to support the language and literacy development of their children. Emphasize the resources that are already an integral part of their home environments, such as telling family stories and speaking, reading, and writing in their home languages. Create a lending library that includes books that reflect the ethnic and linguistic diversity of families. Communicate your ideas with families, for example, create newsletters, videos, or a blog.

13. Collaborate with families to support the language and literacy skills of children with special needs. Establish a method to encourage regular communication about children's daily experiences, such as children's responses to nonverbal cues. For example, create a daily communication book that families can use to record children's progress at home, which they can give to you at the beginning of each day. Record your observations in the book and give it to parents at the end of each day. Use this information to further collaborate with special education professionals.

14. Connect families to online resources, such as family-friendly research-based articles and literacy and language tips. A few suggestions are NAEYC's For Families site (http://families.naeyc.org), Reading Rockets (www.readingrockets.org), and ¡Colorín Colorado! (www.colorincolorado.org).

Identify Resources and Plan Next Steps

15. The resources section (p. 97) contains a rich list of books, articles, and websites related to supporting language and literacy. Select several resources and write annotated descriptions to guide others, perhaps formatting the information as a handout or a web page. Focus the list on an area of interest. For which professionals is the list particularly valuable? For which families?

16. Select an article from this collection or the resources section that supports examples of language and literacy development that are happening in your classroom. Share the key points of the article in a family-friendly manner. For example, create a documentation board using text from the article to support photographs of language and literacy classroom activities.

17. What do you want to know more about in order to better support language and literacy development in your classroom? How can you improve your practices? Create an action plan to guide you, using the practices described in this collection of articles as a model. Identify resources or materials that will help you reach your goals. As you implement your plan, document and reflect on your progress by taking photographs, making audio and video recordings, and/or keeping a journal. Share your insights with colleagues, peers, and families.